RAKE'S PROGRESS

RAKE'S PROGRESS

The MADCAP True Tale of

My Political Midlife Crisis

Rachel Johnson

Alfred A. Knopf · New York · 2021

Library of Congress Cataloging-in-Publication Data
Names: Johnson, Rachel, [date] author.
Title: Rake's progress : the madcap true tale of my political midlife
crisis / Rachel Johnson.
Other titles: Madcap true tale of my political midlife crisis
Description: First American edition. | New York : Alfred A. Knopf,
2021. | Includes index.
Identifiers: LCCN 2020039161 (print) | LCCN 2020039162 (ebook) |
ISBN 9780593318195 (hardcover) | ISBN 9780593318201 (ebook)
Subjects: LCSH: Johnson, Rachel, [date] | Women periodical
editors—Great Britain—Biography. | Periodical editors—Great
Britain—Biography. | Johnson, Boris—Family. | Great Britain—
Politics and government—21st century. | European Parliament—
Elections, 2019.
Classification: LCC PN5123.J65 A3 2021 (print) |
LCC PN5123.J65 (ebook) | DDC 070.92 [B]—dc23
LC record available at https://lccn.loc.gov/2020039161
LC ebook record available at https://lccn.loc.gov/2020039162

Jacket photograph of Rachel Johnson by Dan Kennedy /
The Times Magazine / News Licensing
Jacket design by Keenan

Manufactured in Canada
First American Edition

To Ivo Dawnay

Dawnay was . . . greater than thousands of
baggage camels.

—T. E. LAWRENCE,
SEVEN PILLARS OF WISDOM

.   .   .   .

Logical argument versus emotional argument
equals political defeat.

—DAVID CAMERON, 2019

CONTENTS

I AM KNOWN TO FAMILY AND OLD FRIENDS AS RAKE, WHICH I hope explains my ironic choice of title. My older brother is known to family and old friends as Al, not Boris, which is how he was repurposed at age thirteen after boys at school sacked his room and discovered his passport (and corrected his full name in the document to "Alexander Boris de Pee-Pee Johnson"). I'm afraid I use both names at random in what follows.

Part One

"World King"

TO ADAPT TOLSTOY: ALL FAMILIES ARE SPECIAL, BUT BIG families are—simply by virtue or demerit of their size—more special than standard-issue families just because of this one thing.

There are more of you.

The infinite scope for conflict, friction, jollity, japes, scrapes, fights, and sheer visibility (on a clear day in the U.K. it feels as if you can see and hear the blond tribe of the Johnsons from space) is multiplied exponentially by the number of its members.

No surprise then that large, noisy, public families have a grip on the public imagination. The Mitfords (six daughters, one forgotten son, crazy Farve who hunted his own children to hounds, submissive Mother). The Kennedys. The royal family. The Waltons (as you can sense, I am already running out of famous clans quite quickly before I fasten on my own).

It is a trope that every country regards itself as exceptional, while every child thinks his or her childhood, however peculiar, is normal, because that is all they know.

That wasn't the case in our family. I think we all knew, right from the beginning.

I definitely knew our family was . . . different. From about the age of three I would lie in bed as I heard the grown-up shouts of laughter over those raffia-covered pregnant bottles of cheap Chianti and breathed in their cigarette smoke, thinking, "Why am I part of this family and not another family? How did I end up HERE?"

My parents were in their very early twenties when they started reproducing. Looking back, I can't help measuring my life—and even my adult children's lives—against my parents' own early milestones, even though I realise my mother and father were basically babies when they had babies and that fact alone explains a lot about how things turned out.

"My mother had *three children* by the time she was your age," I said to my oldest son the other day and watched him wince. "When I got pregnant with you, the NHS considered me an elderly primigravida AND I WAS ONLY TWENTY-SIX."

I'm not sure what the point of these comparisons is, but I was always aware that my parents were virtual prodigies because they married straight outta Oxford, had four kids, then divorced seventeen years later.

It was always just assumed that said kids would all go to Oxford and at least one of us—maybe more, my father went on to marry again and have two more children, so I am one of six, and there is no limit to his ambition for his offspring—would become, at the very least, the most important person in the country. (Years ago, people would start asking, "Did your brother always want to be prime minister?" I would answer, "No, he's far more ambitious than that.")

That was always the plan.

· · ·

IN 1970, WHEN I WAS FIVE, A FAMILY FRIEND CAME TO SEE us in Primrose Hill.

Johnson family, sitting room in Primrose Hill, ca. 1972. *Left to right:* Stanley, 32; Rachel, 7; Alexander Boris, 8; Leo, 5.

We lived in two houses in Primrose Hill. The first Johnson residence in NW1 was in Princess Road, bang next to our school, Primrose Hill Primary.

The house was a new-build brick box my mother found easy to clean, or at least easier to clean than our next house in NW1, a crumbling, Victorian, semidetached, stucco-fronted affair opposite the shops on Regent's Park Road, where we moved shortly after my mother had a fourth baby, Joseph, and shortly before my father shunted the whole family to Brussels in 1973 (and then sold Regent's Park Road over the phone to the journalist Simon Jenkins, who'd called to say his current girlfriend, Gayle—a high-maintenance Texas actress who went on to transform my tiny bedroom in the extension into a California-style storage "solution" just for her shoes—wouldn't marry him unless he got our house. My father agreed, as he has never to my knowledge said no to anything. "What was a chap to do?" my father explained. "Simon was, you know, *very keen* on Gayle at the time.").

We weren't in either Primrose Hill or Regent's Park Road long. I remember the latter mainly for the times we left home to go to Casualty.

One day Jo, nine months, consumed some succulent fungus he'd found after crawling behind the washing machine in the basement. His eyes rolled back, he went a funny colour, and my mother had to rush him to University College Hospital, where, as chance would have it, I was already an inpatient, having inhaled eggshell after Al made me choke with laughter over breakfast while I was in the middle of my boiled egg. This resulted in a collapsed lung and pneumonia. I was in hospital so long I did morning lessons on the children's ward and received my own post. All my little classmates were ordered to write me cards. (Maureen wrote, "At School we have been making animals out of flet [*sic*] and I hope you better," and my best friend, Stephen Devaney, wrote, "I'm missing you alot. Specially because of the egg shell in your lung.")

Being in hospital remains one of my happiest childhood memories (my mother, now seventy-seven, gave me the get-well cards but still has the eggshell in a jar that she keeps in a special place along with locks of baby hair and teeth, all to be dealt with in the fullness of time).

"Your baby appears to be high, Mrs. Johnson," the Accident and Emergency doctor said, noting her return without surprise, and took Jo away to have his stomach pumped. (I know how bad this sounds, but don't forget it was the 1970s. As someone commented at length below the line after a piece I wrote for *The Telegraph* about how much I relished my time at prep school—where it was mainly beating, early-morning Greek, and

Left to right: Alexander Boris, 8 (holding baby Joseph, 9 months); Rachel, 7; Charlotte, 30 (holding Leo, 5); Stanley, 32: kitchen, Primrose Hill, ca. 1972.

predatory schoolmasters—today the Johnson children would be taken into care.*)

Anyway, when this family friend paid his visit, Al would have

---

* Here's some of the long comment under the line to my *Telegraph* piece in praise of boarding school:

Rachel's commentary is extraordinarily revealing about her own family background. It is clear from her self-description as a "lumpen parcel" and of her so-called family life in Brussels in the 1970s, that Rachel and her siblings were grossly neglected by any normal standards—emotionally if not materially. Had they come from a different class background and located in Britain they might well have found themselves on the "at risk" register and referred to a social worker. Instead they were rescued by the almost accidental intervention of the European School in Brussels and Father's subsequent decision to follow the advice of an Eton housemaster.

And on it went.

been around six years old. He was born fifteen months before me yet I get furious if people don't know this as I have poured so much time and money into mad, expensive "age-reversal" creams and a punishing fitness and diet schedule, and he very much has not.

In this first memory we were in the downstairs playroom, with its smart modern floor of cork tiles and modular furniture covered with polyester-clad thin foam cushions.

We didn't have a garden, but went to Primrose Hill or used the car park reserved for the other residents of the development, affixed with large signs saying "No Ball Games" and "No Dogs" where we used to play noisy games and thud balls percussively against our neighbours' garage doors. Once, when a man told us to stop, we told on him and my father came out and shouted that if the neighbour told us off again he would "knock his block off"—an act of muscular fatherhood we still remember with admiration and affection to this day.

Down in the playroom, I was in a navy hand-knitted jersey and navy cords and Al was in an identical outfit, only in brown. He might have been sitting in a cardboard box as we were in the middle of a game. We all used to beg him to play games as he made them such fun, but from about the age of ten he would answer, "Okay, let's play reading," which was crushing. Or he would go to his room to stage ancient naval battles in his sink, using corks, pins, and card to re-create the Greek and Persian fleets at, say, Salamis in 480 B.C. (I am genuinely not making this up).

We had no television and never had friends over. Other mothers considered our family "too rough," and as my brother's future wife, Marina, whom we have known since the age of six, confirmed to a biographer years later, we were also "wild and out of control," our "house was always freezing," and furthermore "we all had holes in our socks."

Marina's mother, Dip, stopped her from coming round after my younger brother Leo, aged six, shot Al in the stomach with an air rifle, another red-letter day in the Johnson household. When Al—I guess around nine—was carted to hospital, doctors discovered the pellets had pinged off his dense layer of puppy fat. "I wanted to try and miss Al by a tiny margin to prove I had power of life and death over him," Leo explained when asked why he had shot his brother, "but got him in the middle of the stomach instead." Leo maintains he would do the same today.

In fact, beyond Marina we never really had friends, as we were always moving house or country. As a result we all ended up reading so much that my mother used to shout up to our rooms, "Children! What are you doing?"

"Reading," we would all answer in turn.

"Well, stop reading!" she would shriek.

Left to right: Alexander Boris, 7 (holding cocktail umbrella); Charlotte, 29, holding Leo, 4; Rachel, 6: the downstairs playroom in Primrose Hill, ca. 1971.

Back to Tony, the friend of my parents, who was in a suit in the downstairs playroom.

He knelt to our level and laid his hands on both our blond heads.

"So, children," he said. "Tell me. What do you want to be when you grow up, Rachel and Alexander?" As we gazed up at him from under our thick yellow pudding bowls, cut by our mother with kitchen scissors with towels round our shoulders, we pondered this question.

I tried to think of what women did when they grew up.

My mother was—is—a painter, and a very remarkable one, but I didn't see her like that then. It seemed to me she spent most of her time when she wasn't looking after us smoking or on the telephone or cleaning (a few years later she was admitted to the Maudsley Hospital and stayed there for many long months with a case of OCD so severe that doctors ended up trying, and failing, to cure her with electric shock treatment, which was at least less violent than the other therapy most fashionable at the time: a lobotomy).

I had lots of aunts and uncles: on the maternal Fawcett side, my mother's older sister Sarah was a nun ("Auntie Nun"). Her younger brother, my groovy black-polo-necked uncle Edmund, worked for *Rolling Stone* ("Uncle Monkey"). My mother's two younger sisters were too young to have jobs. My father's three siblings? Hilary was married with children. Peter worked in town planning. Birdie was too young to do anything.

My Fawcett grandmother, a former ballerina, didn't work or eat but was a marvellous cook, and I can taste the crunchy pastry of her buttery Bakewell tart to this day. Granny Butter, my father's mother, was a hill farmer's wife on Exmoor.

It was the first time I had considered the future riddle of grown-up existence. Still, I had just learned to read. My mother taught me with the Ladybird books. *The Little Red Hen, The Hovercraft,* and *Red Riding Hood* are all etched on my memory but none more so than the definitive "Peter and Jane" series published in 1964, foregrounding a tidy, traditional nuclear family in a tidy, traditional suburb of Middle England to prepare the children of Britain for what lay ahead.

Here is Peter and here is Jane. Here is Pat, the dog.

The series starts off reasonably gender-neutral and equal opportunities (the Equal Pay Act was not until 1970), but it all goes Gilead meets *Good Housekeeping* without passing Go by page 6.

Jane is in the kitchen with her mother in a white frock and yellow cardigan, like a mini Princess Lilibet.

Jane likes to help Mummy. She wants to make cakes like Mummy.

"Let me help you, Mummy," she says. "Will you let me help, please? I can make cakes like you."

"Yes," says Mummy. "I will let you help me. You are a good girl."

Meanwhile, Peter was romping with Pat the dog in a Red Indian costume with a feathered headdress, and Daddy was washing the car with a hose.

"We will make some cakes for Peter and Daddy," says Jane. "They like the cakes we make."

I answered first. I had read Peter and Jane. I had done my homework like a girly swot. The future was clear as a windowpane.

"I want to be a wife and mother," I answered. I felt that covered all the available bases.

I remember my father's face. What was wrong with being a wife and mother, like his wife and my mother? I wondered.

His long trips as a white saviour among distant tribes in the Amazon, or exploring in Africa (he called the first volume of his autobiography *Stanley, I Presume?*), or researching his many books about the green revolution or population control in India or China—his contact with his family limited to sending postcards home from Kinshasa or Burundi every so often—had left my prodigiously talented mother no option. She was a tethered brood mare, even though all she wanted to do was paint in her studio that children were never allowed to enter unless she was painting them.

"Alexander?" Tony (Anthony Howard, the editor of the *New Statesman*—I'm pretty sure it was he as there is a picture of this touching tableau in some family album) now turned to my brother.

"World King," he announced confidently, as if he already felt the hand of destiny heavy on his small shoulders. My father nodded with grim satisfaction.

I admit, that shook me. I saw him in a cold, new light. I saw life in a cold, new light. Was that even a job? Could girls apply? I pondered these things in my heart.

That short exchange, folks, was possibly the formative conversation of my childhood.

And his.

That was, in part, how we ended up here.

I did not feel the "hand of destiny" as a small child. Maybe I was the wrong sex, and it was a confidence thing, like all men secretly knowing they can get a point off Serena Williams at tennis, while all women knowing they can't, and all Etonians thinking they can be prime minister.

I can't blame my parents for that. In fact, I am long past the point of blaming them for anything, and never have. As soon as you become a parent yourself, you realise that your mother and father did their level best under impossible circumstances.

In fact, I had it much easier than my brothers. I was the only girl. And I was only a girl. It was my get out of jail free. Nobody expected or wanted me to be World King. Imagine the relief!

But this is not a memoir (please, I am not so delusional as to think I am an Elton John or a Michelle Obama; any memoir will have to wait until I'm at least seventy), more a lightish, three-course meal.

The "mains" in the middle is my abject, absurd, but not entirely ignoble failure to be elected to public office for a new, center-ground, pro-EU political party just as my own brother made his own successful one-man moon shot on Downing Street in July 2019.

However, where relevant, I'll supplement that failure to launch, via this scrambled starter and savoury of childhood and teenage memories. So adjust your sets for yet more flashbacks of grainy, jerky home movies in those saturated 1970s colours. . . .

· · ·

AFTER MY PARENTS' DIVORCE, WHEN I WAS LIVING ALONE for my A levels with my mother in a flat in Ladbroke Grove, she tended to discourage any signs of ambition on my part. She always used to say over family suppers, in front of my three Etonian brothers and any guests crammed around the kitchen table eating her steaming tureens of chili con carne or spag bol, "I've always thought it was a terrible mistake to educate girls."

She didn't literally mean that females should be illiterate.

After all, my mother read English at Oxford, where she met my father and she sat Finals when six months pregnant with me, but her college, Lady Margaret Hall, would insist on addressing her only by her maiden name—Miss Fawcett—even after she became the first married female undergraduate with a baby and another well "on the way."

What she meant was that it was cruel for society to promise equality and not deliver on that promise. I didn't understand at the time that my mother's intention was not to be provocative; she was rather trying to protect me from future disappointment by flagging up the glittering prizes were much more likely to await her three sons than her daughter. She was merely managing my expectations.

If you did educate girls to the same level of boys, she would explain, they would be even more frustrated by their adult lives of indentured servitude to their families, a condition triggered by their own biology that would be supported, enabled, and extended by the men in their lives.

My mother was talking, as you will have spotted long before I did, about herself.

Maddened though I was by this argument as a teenager, it was not until I was pregnant for the third time in four years, aged thirty, that I really saw her point.

My husband worked on Saturdays for a Sunday newspaper, which meant I worked a full week in an office and on Saturday I had the kids on my own and on Sunday too, as he was tired (he was also ill, but that's another story).

I was done in. I craved the simple routine of *Kinder, Küche, Kirche*. I wanted to give up my full-time office job at the BBC and stay at home to look after the children.

Yes, I pined during those fractious Early Learning Centre

years to be a "kept woman" (that is, to live off my husband's modest earnings), do the school run, and take the babies swimming and to the park and to playdates, and I wanted at least an au pair to help me get through the long, long day and the mother's work that was never done.

I felt I was doing it all and doing it badly, but my husband pointed out that we couldn't afford for me not to work full-time.

In fact, the only way we could afford any help at all was if I carried on being a "laying hen." He spelled out my choice: I could work in order to pay for the hours of childcare I had to organise for when I was away at work, or I could be a full-time, hands-on hausfrau on my own.

My father's approach to the problematic issue of childcare was, as he has told many interviewers, to avoid any such conflicts by sending us all away to boarding school as early as possible, even if that meant we lived in different countries for most of the year. He put us down for the best schools as, in his words, "parenting is far too important to be left to parents."

My father also has a fairly binary view of male-female relations. His rule of thumb is to avoid conversation unless absolutely pushed. When it comes to personal relationships, "Never say anything to anybody" is his mantra. But when I was finding it all a strain (the children all had sudden, terrifying illnesses or worrying conditions at various points), he staged an intervention during my protracted childcare crisis.

"But OF COURSE Ivo should pay for you to have help even if you're not out at work," he said, flushing at the thought that one of his daughters was not going to be subsidised to nest at home with some cheery Mary Poppins at her side but had to continue to trek to an office for ten hours a day, leaving his grandchildren to the untender mercies of Polish au pairs. "It's . . . what . . . chaps . . . DO."

But still, I had made my bed.

I remembered how miserable, how bored, my mother's friends were in the 1960s and 1970s, self-medicating "the problem that has no name" with Valium and booze and adultery, with only consciousness-raising groups and copies of *Our Bodies, Ourselves* for recreation. I kept with the conventions of my generation, not theirs. I even kept my maiden name (my husband joked that when the money was coming in, I was Rachel Johnson, but when it was going out, I was Rachel Dawnay).

Many years of graft later I made it into *Who's Who,* and lo! my birthday started appearing in *The Times.* On the first occasion of this mention in despatches, I was having a cosy birthday lunch with my mother in the pub on Ladbroke Road.

"Are you SURE your birthday's in *The Times,* darling?" she said, after I had boasted about it. I fished my paper out of my bag to show her as proof. She peered at the entry and small thumbnail picture.

"But why?" she cried, before congratulating me in wonder, no doubt echoing the reaction of many *Times* readers who cancelled their subscriptions in protest at my inclusion.

2

"We Don't Take Girls, Stanley"

SECOND MEMORY. WE LEFT PRIMROSE HILL IN 1973 AND settled in a large redbrick *villa-avec-jardin* in southeast Brussels in a suburb that the adjective "leafy" cannot begin to do justice. (Uccle was on the lip of a spreading forest called the Forêt de Soignes, and our garden was shaded by tall trees that our father would make us spend entire half terms raking.) We were there because my father was in the first surge of Brits to join the European Commission in the first wave of enlargement. Al, Leo, and I were enrolled in the European School, where the lingua franca was French but we were taught in our native tongues in our national sections while learning how to be good little Europeans—*les bons petits européens*—along with English and maths (possibly interesting data point for nerds: Ursula von der Leyen, the new European Commission president who succeeded Donald Tusk in December 2019, is also a proud alumna, as is my brother's second wife, the aforementioned Marina Wheeler, QC).

It was 1974 and my father was on the telephone to a headmaster in England.

The previous day, the European School had summoned my parents to the campus (a former château on Avenue du Vert

Rachel, Avenue de la Sapinière, Brussels, ca. 1975.

Chasseur in Uccle) to impart the solemn news that after only a few terms they'd ascertained that Al was *doué* (French for "gifted"—I assume I was just average) and declared itself unworthy of the task of educating him. The school had advised my parents that if they were determined to get their boy into Eton, only the jet propulsion of a classical English prep school would do.

This was an admission that the European School's daily curriculum of three-course hot lunch, playing marbles, and beating up the Danes in the playground (always the Danes and never the Germans; the German section was chastened and peaceable) would not cut the mustard for my parents' firstborn son. He was ten, my father was thirty-four, and the headmaster on the blower was Clive Williams of a top Eton feeder school, Ashdown House.

(I still remember the address we used to put on our letters home: "Ashdown House, Forest Row, East Grinstead, Sussex, United Kingdom, The World, The Universe, The Galaxy, The Solar System"—like in *Molesworth,* a seminal text in the Johnson household, along with *Biggles,* Enid Blyton, *Just William, Jennings, The Hardy Boys,* Gerald Durrell, *Asterix, Peanuts,* and of course *Tintin,* to which we were all addicted.)

The Eton entrance exam was only five terms away; we had

never done Hist or Geog let alone Latin or Greek at the European School. In other words, it was panic stations. "That's settled then, Clive," my father said in tones of relieved finality. "Alexander will start next term so you can prep him for Eton"—my father went to the lesser Sherborne School, and he was determined on an upgrade for his sons—"and then there are three more after that!"

You could almost hear the headmaster rubbing his hands at the prospect of all the school fees rolling in. "Ha-ha, send them over," Clive said, chuckling. "Plenty of room at the inn!"

"Then Rachel will start in September," my father said.

There was a pause.

"Ha! Slight snag, Stanley," purred Clive. "We don't take girls."

"Well, you do now, Clive," my father said (the two men were already on first-name terms). "It's all four, or none of them."

I duly went to Ashdown a few months later. This was fine by me.

My parents went out every night, and I minded this, especially after my brother was sent to boarding school and I slept—or tried to sleep—alone in my attic bedroom at the top of the house with its creepy secret passages. I wouldn't be able even to close my eyes until I heard the Opel Kadett drive up to the garage door in the small hours. Sometimes I'd creep down to my parents' bedroom in my despair and leave notes for them to await arrival.

My mother kept all our notes, exercise books, and drawings (as well as our hair and teeth) and gave me all of mine in a clear out a couple of years ago.

This is a note I'd left for them after they'd been out at some wild wife-swapping dinner party (picture *The Ice Storm,* only sadly set in suburban Brussels, not Connecticut).

Dear Mama and Dada

I hope you are not too exhausted. Supposedly there was an English film on but it was in French. I bet you had a fantastic time. Can we have a lie-in demain-matin? I am quite tired. I missed you this evening. Goodmorning (I should think) Rachel

PS Mama, you had better sleep a lot tomorrow.

Part of the problem was that my father had taken us all to see the film *Jaws,* far too soon, as a "treat." I was so traumatised that I had insomnia and anxiety for years thereafter and was even frightened of the water in the WC (my father's other treat was taking us to Baskin-Robbins for ice cream; my mother's comparable best offer was to ask if any of us wanted to accompany her either to the hairdresser or to sit and read in the waiting room while she saw her shrink, a tall, lugubrious, bespectacled Belgian called Dr. Mols).

In the batch of juvenilia my mother gave me was a card I'd made for her around this time.

I'd drawn her with coloured pencils, lying on her back in bed. I'd written the message "Get Better Soon" on the front, and inside I had underlined my plea.

Please get better soon Love Rachel.

With this reasonably bleak home life (on top of the terror engendered by *Jaws,* my mother was in and out of psychiatric clinics) boarding school held few horrors for me.

In fact, boarding school—even an all-boys' one in another country—held only attractions. I had devoured Enid Blyton, and *Molesworth,* so I knew all about boarding school: the dormies, the inedible sossages, the sadistic masters, the howling skool dog. I had always wanted to be a boy and as a child was so furious that I wasn't I refused to wear the tight-sleeved, high-necked Laura Ashley dresses fashionable at the time and insisted on hand-me-down bell-bottom cords and sweaters, determined to be even more macho than my brothers.

Still, Harrods Uniform Department in Knightsbridge had to knock up bespoke costumes of navy pleated skirts and tight nylon turquoise roll-necks that clung to my podgy prepubescent torso just for me and for the one other ten-year-old girl, also the younger sister of an existing pupil.

My two younger brothers followed me. I was the only girl in cricket and rugby teams against other boys' prep schools with the result that, as happened to stuck-up sissies quite rapidly in the Enid Blyton oeuvre, my "corners" were knocked off quite early. The only time I remember my father commenting on a school report, good or bad (I don't think he necessarily read all of them with attention every term, and his proudest boast is that he has never attended a parent-teacher meeting for any of his six children), was when the headmaster's report praised me for making "a couple of crunching tackles" in a rugby match against Brambletye, Ashdown's deadliest rival establishment. "Good stuff, Rake," he said, chuckling over "crunching tackles."

Ashdown was single sex before I got there. It was a feeder school for single-sex Eton, which was a feeder for Oxford, where women—including my grandmother Granny Butter—were not accepted as full undergraduate members until 1920.

I relate this only because it felt that from birth onwards it was natural for me to break ground. I was a female first footer in my mother's womb . . . the family home . . . my all-boys' prep school. Even at university, women were a minority (New College took women for the first time in 1979, five years before I went up). I was the first female graduate trainee at the *FT;* at the Foreign Office, I was the only female in my department apart from the clerks in registry. It was not until I joined the BBC, in 1994, that I had my first woman boss.

No wonder my thought processes at first were a bit unreconstructed when it came to adult existence. Basically, my takeaway from my childhood, education, and upbringing was this: it was all very well for us little ladies to have hobby jobs to keep our hands in as we kept the home fires burning, but the grandeur and gravitas of "statecraft" was reserved for men. And Margaret Thatcher, of course.

In May 1994, I had my first piece published in *The Spectator.* I admit I was thrilled! I felt I'd arrived and was showing off my range when it came to my chosen trade, after years of churning out plodding coverage of government bonds, inflation, and the public sector borrowing requirement for the *FT.* It felt especially good because six weeks before, I had given birth for the second time in fourteen months. Some days I counted it a triumph if I got out of my nightie and made it to the chemist on the corner for yet more barrier cream.

I have one person to thank for this rapid breeding programme. Not my husband and father of my children. And certainly not me.

I was approaching my mid-twenties, I'd been elevated from markets to the "economics room" of the *FT,* I was writing the front-page splash most weeks, whooping it up around town most weekends, unaware of any clock at all. It was then that my mother dropped her bombshell over coffee in the flat we shared (she was making her own living as a painter and took in paying guests as she had refused alimony after the divorce. Money was tight, and she correctly made me pay rent and my share of bills as soon as I left Oxford, which was a great incentive to get on with my life, or at least shack up with a man who had some sort of roof over his head).

"It's all very well having FUN and a CAREER, darling," she said over our industrial-strength Nescafés, "but you mustn't forget a HUSBAND and BABIES." (She never asked about work except to tell me that if a man was annoying me in the office—and it always was a man I was moaning about as there were hardly any women at the paper—I should "make an extra effort to be nice to him.")

I was horrified. My mother was a lefty beatnik free spirit. We were a mixed-race family in every sense (my father tended to marry socialists). My mother, his first wife, painted, taught modern dance, smoked Consulates, walked around in the nude, and displayed her own paintings of her own and my American stepfather Nick's genitalia all over the family walk-up Notting Hill flat we all crammed into after the divorce. But whatever she said must have sunk in. Within a year I had found a man with his own house and was married and pregnant, if not in that order.

When my *Speccie* feature was published in 1994, Anthony Howard, the same man and fêted journalist who had admired my tumbling ringlets in the playroom when I was a little girl, who had asked me what I wanted to be when I grew up, was moved to mark my debut thus. "The only reason Rachel Johnson is published anywhere," he wrote in a *New Statesman* diary piece, "is because she is *Boris's sister*." (My italics.)

I remembered this dig many years later, when another titan of our trade, Paul Dacre, then editor in chief of Associated Newspapers and in theory my boss, said my column in *The Mail on Sunday* "gave banality a bad name" and I, in theory a member of his own staff, wasn't a "real journalist" at all.

Well, then.

In my limited experience, it's only ever older men—trying not to say "the patriarchy"—who lose their shit when women signal a move out of their lane. It arouses in them some reflex to chop us off at the knees with words like "banal," "bossy," and more often "feisty." Men, you will notice, are never feisty. It basically means "You talk too much, woman—shut up."

Which brings us to the point after far too long. Anyone's dismissal makes me all the more resistant to being dismissed. The more I am told to butt out, or mansplained to about how banal or irrelevant I am, the more I want to stick my beak in. I accept this might be genetic.

. . .

THIRD MEMORY. THIS IS ONE OF MY VERY FIRST, IF NOT first, childhood memories, alongside being woken and carried downstairs to sit in front of the TV late one night in 1969 for the moon landings. It was two years before the moon landings, that is, late September 1967, and Al/Alexander and I were waiting in St. John's Wood for my mother and father to bring home our newborn brother, Leo, from hospital. We had pushed a chair up to the sink so we could look out over the taps to the gravelled forecourt of our grandparents' house, where we were camping for a few months, and watch and wait for the Citroën to come home with its exciting cargo of Mama and the fresh new arrival. We stood on the same chair and watched the car swirl around the turning circle and park with a flourish and scatter of gravel. My parents got out. My mother was carrying a white bundle.

My father came into the kitchen with a wicker Moses basket, which he placed on the floor with exaggerated ceremony. We peeked into it. With excited fingers we twitched back the cream silk-edged Lan-Air-Cel blanket (which later became a precious totem called Softy) in the hope of seeing our new baby brother's tiny wrinkled pink face for the very first time.

It was wrinkled, but not in the way we expected. Our father had replaced the baby with a cauliflower.

When new baby Leo was around two, my father said to his then three children (Jo was born in 1971), "Now, don't put baked beans up your noses," as he left the house to go out one evening with my mother. A few days later a foul smell from Leo necessitated yet another trip to Casualty at University College Hospital so that doctors could extract the baked beans that Leo had pushed deep up his own nasal cavities.

Doing what we are told not to do—I have already been forbidden to write this ("No 'World King' stuff please, Rake")—is a family trait.

As is what we call the death wish: the Thanatos urge to say exactly the wrong thing on the *Today* programme, or to do just the thing that will capsize the tiny boat in a storm after the outboard engine has fallen off with your deaf grandmother crying, "Take it, take my life jacket! I've had my life!" as she stares bravely out to sea while we drift towards communist Albania, or to hit the ball miles out of the court during violent games of tennis (my husband calls this affliction Johnsonitis). Essentially, turning everything into either a competition, a game, a joke—or all three.

3

"But Why Don't YOU Go into Politics?"

WHICH BRINGS US, IN A ROUNDABOUT WAY, TO THE CON-
tents of this book.

As two of my brothers were climbing the greasy pole of Parliament and my former politician and environmentalist father
became a late-onset celebrity and the family was never out of
the papers or off the screens, occasionally I'd get lobbed this
question.

"But why don't YOU go into politics, Rachel?"

I'd hear this polite cry during the rolling omnishambles we've
endured since the EU in/out referendum in 2016, but I assumed
it was a courtesy question. Nobody could seriously want more
of us in charge of anything, least of all ME?

I didn't flatter myself that anyone could genuinely think I
could do anything or, as it is fashionable to say now, "make a
difference" to the plight of the sixteen million Remain voters
who have, since the EU referendum, been politically homeless,
unless they turned Lib Dem of course, which, it has to be said,
very few did until the local elections of May 2019, which was
when the yellow tide turned and the latest all-too-brief Lib Dem
resurgence began.

"Me? I voted for the Women's Equality Party," Frances Osborne, the then wife of a former Tory chancellor, George Osborne, told me the morning after she cast her vote in 2019 (the nation has become inured to annual plebiscites).

Given all this, why would I want to go into politics? For a start, there are too many of our family in politics already. *The Times* had anointed the Johnsons—to widespread irritation in the *Guardian*-reading, north London Miliband households, no doubt—"the country's most famous political family."

A recent *Telegraph* mag cover story went with "Britain's Most Political Family." The *Standard*? "The Medicis of West London."

I am sure everyone is bored to tears with us. I am on board with everyone being bored. I would be bored and maddened too. As Giles (brother of Victoria, son of Alan) Coren once said to me, "I'm only the third-best columnist in the Coren family." If I entered politics to spend more time with my family, as the ever-green joke goes, I would only ever be the fourth-most famous politician in the Johnson family after Stanley, Al/Boris, and Jo (I am sensitively listing them in order of seniority).

Leo has shunned the spotlight and moans, "The last thing people want to do is hear about another bloody Johnson. We've got a glut of Johnsons. My dream is to have some sort of Google counter-alert that removes any newspaper article referring to a Johnson."

. . .

AS I AM THE ONLY DAUGHTER OF MY FATHER'S FIRST LITTER, I tended to interpret the "But why don't you go into politics?" question as a backhanded compliment. I assumed my interlocutor thought I would make at least as decent a hash of things as the members of the House of Johnson with a Johnson.

In answer, though, I would laugh. Not going into politics was one of my lifetime red lines, like not learning how to play golf or having any "work" done on my face. I understood why other people were compelled to do it, but it was something I felt I could swerve and somehow, somehow, the sun would still rise in the morning.

And then.

Rewind to the run-up to the referendum. February 2016.

I had spent the day in Al's farmhouse in Thame trying to persuade him to back David Cameron and not campaign against his own prime minister for Leave. His decision had to be made the following day, Sunday, in a column to be filed to *The Daily Telegraph* for publication that coming Monday.

We played tennis in the rain, and over the net I shouted scenarios for what would happen if Leave or Remain won as we hit soggy balls at each other before repairing indoors for burnt lasagne washed down with red burgundy. After lunch we sat by a hissing fire, me reading his two columns: one advocating Remain, the other Leave, on his laptop.

"It's clear to me that the Remain one is compelling," I said, as texts pleading for him to be loyal from George Osborne, the chancellor, and the PM, David Cameron, pinged into his buzzing phone, which trembled on the windowsill, ignored.

"The long one for Leave is all about nebulous stuff like control and sovereignty, and the only tangible benefit you point to is this long section"—I jabbed at the screen—"all about how if we leave, you will be able to change the height of drivers' wing mirrors and perhaps stop young women on bikes being smushed under the wheels of lorries turning left in London. Is that really it?"

I also tried, "Just look at the scaly lineup of Leavers," then listed them. "Galloway! Banks! Farage! Um, okay, Gove is a good get for the outers, but do you really want to be with that lot, not the in crowd?"

"If you don't know what to do, do the right thing," texted Cameron.

Short digression: Cameron was in the year below me at university; I had met him socially and got on with him. At a Notting Hill function he was introduced by my blond half sister, Julia, a teacher, to my blond half brother, Max. He recoiled as if scalded. "No!" he yelped. "Not another one! However many more of you are there?"

I had to make a public apology to the then PM in 2014 when I had taken my laptop to work in a bitcoin café in Shoreditch and had popped to the loo, leaving my laptop on the table. When I came back and resumed my article about living cashless for a week for British *Vogue,* I started getting worried calls.

"Are you okay? I think your Twitter's been hacked," friends informed me.

I jumped onto Twitter, where it appeared that I had sent a tweet, which was being retweeted dozens of times a second.

"Why is David Cameron such an egg-faced cunt?" my @rachelsabihajohnson account had asked a few minutes earlier, to the manifest delight of shadow ministers who said they were grateful to me for asking this and would bring up this important matter at Prime Minister's Questions in the Commons the next day. Others objected to my tweet on the grounds that "he has a face like a bum, not an egg."

Two years later, that little episode felt far away and long ago and almost innocent as the country stared down the barrel of the referendum Cameron had so unwisely thrust upon us and my brother had to choose which way to jump within the next twenty-four hours.

"Your choice will be one we all have to live with," I said,

piling into an old box of Belgian chocolates I had found under a drift of newspapers. "If you make a wrong choice, it won't be just you who suffers; it could be the entire country. The column you send," I told him pompously, "could crash the Continent." At that stage, with the migration crisis, the euro crisis, the rise of populism, it was felt that if the U.K. left, there would be contagion and Italy and Greece could follow suit and then . . .

"If it goes wrong, it's not just a disaster for YOU. It's a disaster for us all, and our children's children," I concluded.

Before I left Oxfordshire, I said to Al that I thought the country would vote for the status quo and therefore he would be on the losing side.

"I don't give a fuck about being on the losing side, the wrong side of history," he insisted. "I only care about doing the right thing."

"In that case," I said as I got into the car in the drizzle, "go for it." I couldn't think what else to say. He seemed genuinely agonised.

I texted Marina, Al's then wife. "He'll need balls of steel," I said.

Marina Wheeler, of course, was the power behind the throne and had made her principled disapproval of the long interfering arm of the European Court of Justice in spiky legal blogs, often reprinted by the Leave-leaning *Spectator*. She was an ur-Brexiteer. It seemed to me that my brother was impaled on the horns of a dilemma. He did not just have to choose between Leave and Remain. He had to choose between his wife and his boss.

The next day he came out, as I knew he would, for Leave. Marina, Gove, Farage, Banks, Cummings, you name it, had all prevailed against me and Ivo, not to mention his chancellor and his prime minister, the Confederation of British Industry, the governor of the Bank of England, the president of the United States, J. K. Rowling, and David Beckham. Basically the entire establishment—from 74 per cent of elected MPs to the Liverpool manager, Jürgen Klopp—said we should stay and were stronger together, which, in retrospect, goes some way to explaining the campaign's stunning Viking victory. It was an up yours to the Man.

Cameron was furious.

"OUT for Himself" was the headline in *The Independent,* while in the Commons a hopping mad PM reacted to the betrayal like a Sicilian woman scorned.

"I have no other agenda than what's best for the country," the PM stormed at the despatch box.

I thought then that my brother's judgement had failed him on this basis. There was no deal that we could ever do with the EU that would be better than the one we already had. I felt he had backed the wrong side, quite possibly not for entirely self-less reasons. But his ratlike nose for power—and channelling the sublime instincts and soaring desires of the British people—could not ever be doubted.

· · ·

ON REFERENDUM DAY, JUNE 23, 2016, I VOTED, THEN FLEW to Cannes, where I was doing a speaking event about the referendum and the EU for the *Mail Online* for my then paymasters, Associated Newspapers. The other speakers were the right-wing demagogue Katie Hopkins and my fellow *Mail* columnist Richard Littlejohn, also very right wing.

After our event I went back to my hotel to watch the news roll in. I stayed up all night, past the Sunderland result, until an ashen and grizzled David Dimbleby confirmed the historic upset at dawn. (A couple of years later I bumped into Noel

Gallagher—the pop star—and he told me he'd gone to bed straight from the recording studio that night. "I went to sleep assuming nobody would vote Leave," he told me. "I woke up and the world had changed.")

As the Brexiteers on the Riviera—mainly at the outsized Associated Newspapers gin palace—whooped and hollered and cheered, I left my hotel on the promenade and watched the sun rise.

On the plane back to London I wrote a long piece for *The Mail on Sunday* for that weekend. What I wrote was this—and, by the by, isn't it sad that tosh I write for a tabloid is no longer tomorrow's chip wrapper but lives forever online, while shimmering, precise prose published between hard covers has the half-life of a mayfly?

Anyway, herewith an extract of my piece written on June 24, 2016, the morning after the referendum, just hours after the PM, David Cameron, had resigned, whistling a merry tune, and walked offstage to write his memoirs in a £25,000 shed:

> If a week is a long time in politics then it's a lifetime in my family. And what an astonishing, upsetting, stunning week it has been, a stinging reminder that no politician should ever ask the public a question he doesn't know the answer to. Now the snow globe is not just shaken but lying broken on the floor.
>
> A week ago today my father was addressing the Remain rally in Hyde Park while my brother was headlining the one for Leave in Billingsgate. Afterwards we all went to Boris's birthday party hosted by our brother Jo in Camden.
>
> There were toasts (if we brought presents, I forget what they were) and, of course, a very few "well-chosen

words" from Boris about what was going on, but nothing to frighten the horses. He was interrupted by my Remainer husband Ivo shouting: "Brexit . . . pursued by a bear market."

It was business as usual, but I thought I sensed a rare despondence emanating from the then leading light of Leave. Everyone was calling it for a narrow Remain victory, a result that suited almost all of us.

What a fool I was. As I watched the news all night, as area after area consciously uncoupled from the EU, it rammed home the truth. I live in an insulated, isolated golden bubble along with the pampered townie elites. I accept with appropriate humility that this, the loudest of fanfares for the common man, is a deafening raspberry to people like me, who have never felt the sharp end of mass immigration, only profited from it, while displaying contempt to the communities ignored by London and Westminster.

In the cold light of Independence Day 2016, I could see with perfect hindsight that my lot had this latter-day Peasants' Revolt coming.

If anyone is going to give Boris the benefit of every doubt, it's me. But I have to write and say this anyway. The polls were wrong. The markets were wrong. The bookies were wrong. The pundits were wrong. But—although we can't say the people were wrong, damn them—this still feels wrong to my stomach.

I understand the fury of people who can't get appointments at their GPs' surgeries or their children places in primary schools.

But when the BBC called it for the take-control freaks,

as dawn spread over sea and the super-yachts squatted in the harbour, I went down to the beach and, by the shores of the Med, I sat down and wept.

When I went in to breakfast, all the Brits were sitting around, stunned, staring into their bowls of café au lait. They were even talking to strangers, such was the shock. A woman stopped at my table. "Yesterday I pitched that our agency should be the European hub of Intel," she said to me, shaking her head. "Today we're not even European."

. . .

AND ON THE PIECE WENT. IT APPEARED THE SUNDAY AFTER the referendum, and I have not stopped making the pro-EU case since. In print, on telly, at dinner tables, in the street, on buses—so much so that I have begun to bore myself. After a certain point, though, I felt that "making the case" was not enough.

Yes, while the suffragettes threw themselves in front of the king's horse or chained themselves to railings or women's libbers burnt their bras, I did something more sensational: I joined the flatlining, post-coalition, "toxic" (as they were back then) Lib Dems, an act of sheer political courage that everyone laughed their heads off to my face about for years.

For once, I had done something my husband approved of (he had joined the party even earlier in 2017). "It's been 25 years since my wife @Rachelsjohnson and I agreed on anything—but then Brexit," Ivo tweeted. "I joined the Lib Dems 6 weeks ago. Why haven't you?"

At the time they were the only party that had a sensible policy on Brexit: a second referendum giving voters the chance to at least inspect the new house before they torched the old one (it was only under their ill-fated and short-lived leader Jo Swinson that they pivoted to their doomed "Revoke" posture). The "story" of my joining the Lib Dems before the general election of 2017 was broken by Cathy Newman of *Channel 4 News* and Jane Martinson of *The Guardian* simultaneously (I had blabbed it to both of them myself at an awards lunch), and they had agreed to share the spoils.

"The foreign secretary's sister Rachel has become a member of the Lib Dems, and has even held talks with the party about standing in one of its target seats in the South West as a parliamentary candidate in the election," the report ran.

"Mr. Johnson was the most prominent Brexiteer, and without him many in the Leave campaign believe they would have lost the referendum in June. But his decision to back Brexit caused a family rift, with Ms. Johnson writing about how she and her children cried after the referendum result with her nineteen-year-old son Oliver telling her 'Uncle Boris has stolen our futures.'"

I'm afraid the news was deemed notification-worthy (it was one of those "breaking" flashes that appears on your phone), and I therefore fielded pained queries from friends who had been driving or at work as to why their days should be interrupted with a portentous notification that a fifty-something journalist had joined a soggy-bottomed center party.

Cathy Newman's payoff explained it, of course.

Her piece ended: "The foreign secretary could not be reached for comment."

Marina, my sister-in-law, was not happy. "Why couldn't you just join quietly and not say who you were going to vote for like everyone else?" she said. It did not go down well in their house. Not at all well.

"You have to resign from the Lib Dems immediately," my brother ordered. "I am getting blowback on the doorstep about it! Rake!" he spluttered.

"This is NOT THE STUFF TO GIVE THE TORY TROOPS."

But joining the Lib Dems was the price I felt I had to pay to put clear blue water between me and the true Be-Leavers. I couldn't join the Lib Dems under cover of darkness, nor did I want to. I wanted to get stuck in.

After Cameron called the referendum, the basic sequence of headline events as far as I'm concerned went like this. Michael Gove got my brother over the line to lead the Leave campaign. My brother got the country over the line to vote Leave, and it has been a bloody nightmare ever since.

Politics is politics and family is family. That will never change. Family will always come first. But whenever someone puts up "write a sad/funny story in three words" on Twitter, I am tempted not to write "my phone died" or "she left me" like the others but "sister of Boris." I never have, as I hate the traitor-sister narrative, but what he did changed the course of history. It felt like a compass error, harder to correct with every mile travelled, and just as Cameron played Russian roulette with the country and—as the writer Robert Harris judged—"blew its brains out," I worried my brother was stuck in that Bruce Springsteen song. He had a hungry heart, but he took a wrong turn and just kept going.

Maybe that's too brutal. But what is true is that Brexit—or the vote to Brexit—radicalised the entire country. I literally can't think what we all fought about before.

Stanley and my brothers Jo and Leo and I all campaigned to remain in the EU. My father co-chaired, with Baroness Young of Old Scone, a pressure group called Environmentalists for Europe in 2016.

Still, he reserved the right to edit his position as events unfolded.

"I said, I am a Remainer, but the country voted to leave and as a democrat I must support Brexit," he flip-flopped in an interview last year with the Brexit-supporting *Telegraph.* "You may say it's my life's work—my life in the European Commission and the European Parliament—going down the drain. But this is the way the country has voted."

Stop there for a moment to consider this, then—whether the U.K.'s decision to leave the EU was actually the expression of a private Oedipal struggle in one family, only played out on a continental scale. A father's lifework, dumped off by his oldest son . . .

I agree—a far-fetched notion, not even worthy of a Jeffrey Archer potboiler. But what is unarguable is this. From never having given the EU a moment's thought (in 2006, only 3 per cent of voters named Europe as an important issue, compared with 38 per cent who nominated the NHS; in 2015, only 1 per cent thought that membership of the EU was the most important issue facing the country), since Boris created Brexit, the *And God Created Woman* moment of British politics, we talked of nothing else for three years.

The BBC news channel or Sky News became the new reality TV. I read blogs from the London School of Economics about the sectoral impacts of no deal or a long thread on Twitter about the World Trade Organisation from a professor of Brexit studies from Birmingham rather than the new Jilly Cooper in bed.

In June 2019, I was at an event with the BBC's Europe correspondent Katya Adler—she was receiving an award—and I felt as if I were in the presence of some Hollywood screen goddess or deity. She shimmered in her violet dress as her disciples tried to touch the hem of her raiment, or just stare at her.

If you want to hook up with someone in the U.K., you no longer send the traditional booty call. Since the referendum, the election, and the rolling maul of news that has consumed us, a far more alluring invitation is "BBC Parliament channel and chill?"

· · ·

BUT COME 2017, MY NEW PARTY, THE LIB DEMS—LET'S FACE it—were not moving the dial. Whatever the question, they were not the answer. They were not capable of preventing this national act of self-harm, or talking down this country from committing economic suicide, not on their own. They were tainted over tuition fees, tainted over their joint commission of austerity with the Tories (so tainted officials spent years processing the returned membership cards that many, many Lib Dems sent back after coalition). I had the sense that my public stance—which had expended my personal and professional capital as my family and employers sneered—was pointless and painful. It was both too much and not enough.

I am secretly a medium-serious person. Secretly, like everyone else, I long to be taken more seriously. That, I acknowledge, means taking myself more seriously. And I was—still am—seriously worried about the dangerous politics of the accommodation of the Far Right. The bad economics of a no-deal Brexit.

I was seriously worried about the post-fact, post-truth, post-shame environment where politicians trade only in lies and nobody calls them out on their lies.

I was seriously worried about Nigel Farage, a man who was making millions of angry people even angrier by persuading them that the EU stole their sovereignty and Parliament stole their democracy and telling them only he can give them their country back.

And I was worried that the then leader of our country, Theresa May—and the next, before her successor's thumping general election success in December 2019—was initially voted in by a tiny selectorate of old white men in the South East of England (trying not to say "gammon"). The 160,000-strong Tory membership, average age fifty-seven, was 71 per cent male and 97 per cent white. It comprised, in total, 0.3 per cent of the electorate. Break it down, and basically it was as if the red-trousered members of the MCC had convened in their egg-and-bacon-striped ties in the Long Room at Lord's and decided who should run the country. (Even Vladimir Putin, of all people, was to mock us for this when my brother was running to be PM. Imagine.)

At my back I was always (in the Milton poem it is spelt "alwaies") hearing not Time's winged chariot, but the cries of my unborn grandchildren. "What did YOU do during Brexit, Grandma, when that man Farage was trying to take the country back to the 1930s?"

Given we all know what happened in Europe in the last century, how could I stand idly by as judges were called enemies of the people; as Remain MPs were trashed as traitors or saboteurs; as diplomats and civil servants—even soldiers—were treated like collaborators in Vichy France, tarred and feathered in the Brexit press day after day. Everyone and anyone was thrown under the bus if they baulked at being willing executioners of an instruction—the sempiternal referendum result in 2016—they believed would only make the country poorer and more insignificant.

Europe has been the graveyard of every Tory prime minister from Margaret Thatcher to Theresa May. It will bury more in years to come as Brexit consumes everything—and everyone—like hot lava in its path. I lie in bed, worrying that nobody will get out of this one unscathed.

There has been no agenda but Brexit, even in the last two (2017, 2019) general elections. Brexit sops up all the juice of the government and the civil service, despite the fact that it was—pick your metaphor—a piece of Ikea furniture that the country had ordered online, which arrived in an outsized cardboard box, minus instructions and with key bits missing, as well as lacking the right tools for assembly. Instead of sending it back, Parliament has spent three years trying to post it through the letterbox.

The cry would go up, at intervals, during all this. Why could the land of the Chelsea Flower Show, of the Trooping of the Colour and the Wimbledon tournament, of the immaculate state occasion, of the mother of parliaments, of the inventor of all the best ball games, why could this land not coddle and nurture in our national allotment some homegrown boy wonder during this epic shitstorm to lead us out of this mess? (Or even girl wonder, but that's a tougher call. Pressure groups from Women 2Win to 50:50 have tried to plug the political gender gap, but between 1918 and 2015 only 450 women have been elected as members of the House of Commons, which is fewer than the total number of men in the 2015 Parliament; in the Lords, men outnumber women three to one.) Where, the moderates wailed, was the U.K.'s version of En Marche, which swept to the Élysée after only six months? Who would be the British Macron?

On February 18, 2019, it seemed that our bootless cries were at last answered.

4

"When Are You Going to Do Anything Except Appear on Television?"

STEP FORWARD THE FEARLESS TIGGERS (AS THEY WERE THEN called), a name created from their bouncy acronym TIG, standing for the Independent Group. MPs Chuka Umunna, Mike Gapes, Ann Coffey, Angela Smith, Chris Leslie, Gavin Shuker, and Luciana Berger left the Labour Party on February 18, with Joan Ryan the following day. Anna Soubry, Heidi Allen, and Sarah Wollaston left the Conservative Party on February 20, and together they formed a big-tent, joined-up party for defectors from the two main parties.

It was hailed as a mass prison break of politics! Rash comparisons were made to the foundation of the SDP and the Gang of Four, who split from the Labour Party in 1981.

Our brave, bold Tiggers made their mark from the off. In response to their creation, Sir Keir Starmer, the Labour Brexit secretary and future leader of the party, went more pro-Remain and more anti–no deal and started talking up Labour's move to a second referendum. The splitters spawned a party within a party, led by Tom Watson, to neutralise the appeal of the rebel alliance and to forestall a further exodus to join the new kids on the block. Within days, Theresa May said no deal was off the table.

And so Chuka Umunna set out his stall: the "old" and "main" parties could not be the change because they had become the problem, he said. No leadership, no direction, divided, incompetent, putting party before national interest, unrepresentative of the "complex tapestry" of modern Britain.

All this spoke to me. It stirred my blood.

Now a bunch of prospectors of new horizons were staking a claim to higher middle ground. They had no infrastructure, no party machine, no data, and would have to build it all from scratch, but I didn't know that yet. I felt a shiver down my spine.

In big moments I never feel the hand of destiny. Instead, I feel condemned to endure some inescapable and punitive sentence, like agreeing to have everyone for Christmas.

In fact, I felt just as I did when my father introduced me to a divorcé thirteen years older than me at a business lunch in Rio de Janeiro on a steamy New Year's Day in 1990. Even though Ivo was pouring sweat and was replacing his own body fluids with bottomless caipirinhas, I had this sinking feeling that I was going to marry him.

If you build it, do they come? Would I come? Far more important, would anyone else come? Those were the questions.

I hesitated. I've never done politics, and I am fifty-three years old. I identify as a wife and mother at heart, as per my reflex childhood responses to Tony and others.

More to the point: my mother was a grandmother six times over at my age. I am entering the era of slippers and roses and the *Antiques Roadshow*.

Not to mention this. It was scary out there, back in early 2019, and getting scarier by the minute as the Olympia exhibition center—capacity ten thousand—overflowed with nationalists for rallies, as if we were rerunning the 1930s, and genteel rural music festivals were threatened if they even dared to play Beethoven's "Ode to Joy," Europe's anthem, as if that were an act of cultural treason.

Second, I am a fervent and noisy Remainer. Given my primary role in public life as "Boris's sister" (newspapers caption photos of me "Rachel Johnson, sister of Boris" as if it were my day job, like being a plumber, rather than an accidental side hustle of biology), everything I say about politics is portrayed as unpatriotic disloyalty to the one-man Juggernaut of Brexit, the Dark Lord of Leave, rather than an expression of my own, deeply held, personal opinions.

The *Express*—a right-wing daily—has a team of reporters who stalk and track my every move and utterance so they can run stories titled "Rachel Johnson BRUTALLY Shut Down by Patriotic Brexiteer as She DEFIES Will of the People" and variants of that headline every five minutes.

The referendum result didn't just dog whistle the yearning to boomerang us back to a time when nobody had the temerity to speak foreign languages on trains, and no EU citizens treated our country "as their own." It was a hunting cry licensing xenophobia for general use that carried from one end of the country to another.

On top of all that, there's Twitter and Facebook and WhatsApp. Social media. All of it serves as a toxic petri dish for anonymous onanists in their underpants to generate grisly insults from their childhood bedrooms, such as the man who said, "Most of my str8 friends would prefer to shag Boris than Rachel" (and trust me, that is one of the kinder ones).

Meanwhile, I have—or had, until my moment of spring madness—a nice life.

I make—or made—a modest living writing articles about my

bum or my hair or composing gentle features about the life cycle of the Norland nanny, and doing debate shows on telly, and I like to spend as much of my time as possible on the tennis court.

I have—or had—no wish to leave the Fourth Estate for the pugilistic Pugin corridors of the parliamentary estate, let alone Brussels.

It is true that at around that point—I think one brother was foreign secretary, another was transport minister, and my main gig was doing a debate show on Sky News and writing columns—Al wondered out loud, "Rake. When are you going to do anything except appear on television?"

He wasn't the only one to ask such a thing. When I went to Lord's to watch the cricket that summer, I bumped into Jeffrey Archer.

"When are you ever going to do a proper job?" he demanded, just as my old English teacher Miss Gough, who went on to become the high mistress of St. Paul's, asked me when I saw her in the street many years later, "When are you going to publish a *real* book?"

Well. In my defence, m'lud, though it may look as if I have put decades of hard yards into only being an underachiever and not being taken seriously, I have published to date seven books! I have edited *The Lady,* a genteel magazine of unimpeachable fragrance based in Covent Garden! Above all, I have kept the show on the road! When such blows rain down, I want to bleat out my CV—*FT,* BBC, Foreign Office, and so on—but don't. I submit to their higher authority. After all, when you have two brothers in government, being important public servants while you are the unremunerated slave of your family and dog, you feel you don't have much to write home about. You don't have the prefix Right Honourable before your name or MP after it. You don't officially exist.

But still, in private, I admit such accusations that I have wasted my entire life sting a little.

I am reminded of the time my father was asked in my presence—some television greenroom, a few years ago—if he could list all his six children and their occupations in order. He answered in the affirmative with misplaced confidence and cantered off.

"Boris is mayor of London; Jo is an MP; Leo is a sustainability expert and partner at PWC," he began, ticking us off his fingers. "Julia is a singer and head of Latin at her school; Max is at Goldman Sachs in Hong Kong . . ." and then he trailed off.

"That's five. There must be one more," he said. Then his face cleared.

"Oh yes, there's Rachel," he said, beaming. Pause. What could he say to impress his rapt audience? I wondered. Would he say that I've been a journalist and broadcaster since the age of twenty-three, even that I was jointly awarded the Bad Sex in Fiction Award with John Updike, and won *Pointless Celebrities*?

No.

"Rachel"—my father cast about in desperation—"Rachel has very good teeth."

That was basically where we were until 2016. The others did things he could show off about, while I've never had a filling (true). I made a living as a freelance (in fact, some called me a "prolific" or "ubiquitous" media tart, never considered an excellent thing in a woman). I kept house. I was a good daughter, wife, and mother, or at least not a bad one. I walked the dog.

Now fast-forward, friends, Remoaners, countrymen, to April 2019. Having "unjoined" the Lib Dems a few weeks before, I had registered my support for Chuka's bold start-up, upstart, pop-up party. These Tigger MPs were brave. They had given up everything to provide folk like me with an alternative. They would not tolerate the spreading poison of racism, or nativism, in their parties. They seemed nice, almost cool even. Above all, they weren't the Lib Dems!

All it took was clicking one mouse. I did it.

I was postmenopausal. Nothing scared me anymore.

I didn't care if there was milk in the fridge or what my family was having for supper. The oestrogen had left the building. My guilty pleasure was throwing things out. I had no "caring hormones" left in the endocrine system at all. It felt not so much like my time as the time to act.

How dare boys I'd known in short trousers at prep school and university YUP, I would rage, how dare these SQUITS decide that my children and grandchildren couldn't work, live, love, and travel across Europe as freely as we had? How dare my peers take away from my own children freedoms and opportunities they themselves had enjoyed?

Come April, the European elections that were never supposed to happen were weeks away. The PM couldn't get her deal over the line. Meanwhile, Nigel Farage's new Brexit Party was doubling in size every five minutes, rallying crowds across the country, and Brexit Party tweets were spamming my timeline.

I got a DM from Dan Hodges, the *Mail on Sunday* columnist. "I feel as if I'm living through the Thirties," he said.

Then I got an email that was the season opener of the three or four weeks that did not change the world. It was from Change UK, and it was addressed to all their supporters. The subject line was "European elections." Although there was no pressure whatsoever for the fledgling groupuscule to contest a national election, the decision was taken to field candidates and fight. Every seat.

You had to admire the pluck.

(Tedious but important footnote: The Tiggers had registered as a political party with the name Change UK. Everyone in the Bubble—shorthand for the Westminster media-political complex—liked the catchy bounce of the name Tiggers. At least it made the group sound fun and frisky, but the electoral commission, not for the first or last time, put a fatal spoke in the wheel. When the party tried to register as TIG, they were told that—as if enrolling for political Equity—the name Independent had already been taken. They became Change UK, which everyone apart from our leader in all but name, Chuka Umunna, thought was terrible. It can be shortened, of course, to Ch UK, which sounds like a convenient personal vehicle for him. There was also the little problem of the petition website Change.org, which said it would sue Change UK if they used the name— every time they used the name. Finally, the two entities came to an agreement that Change.org would lend the name for the election period only. Suboptimal, I agree.)

Anyway, Change UK asked us all if we wanted the honour of representing the party as candidates in the forthcoming Euro elections. They were looking for seventy candidates to field full slates of prospective MEPs across the regions. Lo, several thousand supporters, including me, did want the honour.

Ivo and I were in Jamaica, staying at a Sandals resort in Montego Bay with excellent Wi-Fi. The form was straightforward. It luckily didn't leave a lot of space for me to trumpet my achievements, which was a relief as I didn't really have any. I explained my passionate position vis-à-vis the U.K. leaving the institution that, though baggy and windy, had stopped us being the sick man of Europe and had kept us in peace and prosperity for as long as I have been alive. As I typed, my eyes prickled with tears at the futility and stupidity of the proposition both of the main parties had vowed to execute.

When asked which region I wanted to represent I ticked London and the South West, as that is where I live. I completed the form, plus a PDF of my CV—which is still the apogee of my adult technical achievement—and pressed send. I didn't bother mentioning it to Ivo, as I thought nothing would come of it.

This led to something of a marital as Ivo announced that very lunchtime at the jerk chicken shack that he had also applied to be a candidate. I didn't confess immediately that I had done so too. There seemed no point in having the row. Sending the form back was, I assumed, a classic futile gesture: I was applying to stand for a party that had only been in existence a fortnight to contest elections that were not supposed to happen. After all, we should have left the EU on March 29, precisely in order to avoid having to stand U.K. candidates for the European Parliament elections on May 23. I thought Mrs. May would do anything she could to stop them. Not for the first time, I was wrong.

A brief note on the marital that my Euro election application triggered.

Ivo was far crosser about my applying to be a Euro MP than he was when I broke the news to him that I was going to enter the *Big Brother* house in 2018 and appear on reality TV for weeks on end and be filmed like an animal in a zoo. "I'll divorce you if you do *Big Brother,*" he said when I told him I was going to do the show.

Then I told him how big the cheque was. "I'll divorce you if you don't," he said, beaming.

Still, I knew he would kick up. The only three things we have ever agreed about in the course of a long—twenty-six-year— marriage were these:

- the Christian name of our firstborn son, Ludovic
- the fact that *The Night Manager* starring Tom Hiddleston was underwritten and overrated
- the horror of Brexit

Indeed, our united front over the referendum result in 2016 was a bonding experience for us as a couple to such an extent that we sometimes joke that "Brexit saved our marriage." But he was still peeved. My husband claimed—actually, still does—that I only sent in my form when he said he was going to apply solely in order to "upstage" him. (Tsk. When has a Johnson ever done anything simply to get attention? People can be so unfair!)

I assumed he wouldn't fill in the form in Jamaica and send it back.

I assumed there would never be Euro elections in 2019.

In neither case was this a correct assumption.

In mitigation, these were not—are not—normal times.

· · ·

I'LL NEVER FORGET WHAT MY MOTHER SAID WHEN I HAD three children under four. I was jangling with boredom, exhaustion, and caffeine-fuelled frustration. By the time Oliver came along in 1996, I had chucked in a staff job at the BBC I adored to go freelance and, as they say in the United States, "do kids." Much as I loved every single inch of my children and would have killed anyone who so much as harmed a hair of their blond heads, I found I missed the deep, deep peace and professional satisfactions of the office compared with the intense, high-octane, stressful, demanding hurly-burly of the nursery world.

Now I was feeding and mopping up and bathing on a loop, interspersed by heart-stopping mercy dashes to the hospital (one child had severe epilepsy I am still too traumatised and protective to talk about more than two decades later, another had terrible asthma and eczema, while my youngest turned out to be so blind that he never saw clouds until he was three years old, at which point he got bottle-bottom glasses and asked, "What are those white things in the sky?").

To me they were, and are, absolutely perfect and precious in every way, and when a friend and mother of six strapping progeny once asked me how I felt about having "defective children," I never spoke to her again.

I didn't, I admit, find childcare and housework quite as serene and photogenic as I expected from my quick flicks through the Mini Boden catalogues lying around the houses of my friends who'd already had babies. This publication would plop onto my doormat and showed mummies and "kiddies" (copyright the Duchess of Cambridge) romping barefoot on golden Norfolk beaches in chinos and something called "lamby" funnel-necked fleeces, as buff, rugged daddies boiled tea in iron kettles over campfires picturesquely located next to bunting-strewn and battered Land Rover Defenders.

This was not, I feel I should warn prospective parents now, adequate preparation for having children in my twenties. While my peers of both sexes climbed career ladders or greasy poles (that is, took coke and shagged strangers they had met in nightclubs under the Westway or went to three-day music festivals), I worked full-time and went home to my second job, my children.

Most of the time, I just got on with it, feeling incredibly lucky to have them all and a job, but I craved sleep, time to read, time to think, which is why I always made sure the children had these two key skills by about aged two: how to turn on the TV and how to operate the video recorder.

My mother—who had it so much harder than I did; she was once buried alive on Exmoor on her in-laws' hill farm without a car, dishwasher, or washing machine for a whole year—would hear me out as I mithered on about my stalling career and how tired I was and then say, "No experience is ever wasted."

She was right. She is right. The poo-nami of having children—and also, being one of so many siblings I considered calling this book *Birth Order*—was actually a perfect preparation for the shitshow that is dipping a toe into politics.

Her other classic watchword is "it is urgent to do nothing" when faced with a crisis or as we term it now a life challenge. Do nothing is almost always the best and safest course of action. Obviously, this doesn't apply to a child having a life-threatening epileptic fit requiring ventilation or resuscitation, or managing to lock a six-month-old baby and the only available car key for the vehicle simultaneously in a Dodge minivan during a 120-degree heat wave in Washington, D.C. (both crises I have coped with), but it is good value in most other eventualities.

But when the whole country was going bonkers, shouty-crackers over Brexit, I felt I could not stand by and shrug, flick over the channel, and turn the page.

It was urgent to do something.

In the next chapters, there follows the sorry tale of how I broke ranks with the unspoken compact to leave the men to public office and briefly entered politics but left it feeling as if I'd been part of an extinction event, and all at the exact same time my older brother mounted a final assault on the summit of his lifetime ambition, Downing Street.

Here is the story of the Tiggers/the Independent Group/Change UK and my bit part in its downfall.

How I managed to cross all the red lines and cardinal rules of campaigning—and in record time.

How the week before polling day, the head office was cancelling my national media appearances.

How, as the campaign unfurled, one brother in Parliament was telling me he assumed I was a "sleeper cell" for the Brexit Party, and the other was hailing my campaigning skills as "politics as performance art."

How the party itself crossed all the red lines too when it comes to starting a new party: no money, tick; no agreed policies, tick; no organisation, tick; no consensus among the top team, tick; no leader, tick tick tick—all the way up to one of the leaders openly calling on voters not to vote for us and back other parties on the eve of Election Day.

Here is the inside story of how and why, after a lifetime spent in a political family but after only a month in politics, I fully expected to be shot by the apparatchiks of the former nu-Labour Politburo of Chuka Umunna at dawn after the declaration in Poole on May 26, 2019.

Here is the inside story of how the party itself imploded around me and will go down in the annals as the fastest collapse in party political history.

At first people said, "Gosh, you're brave." Then it was, "At least you might have some fun" and "It'll make a change."

A week before polling it was, "It'll be over soon, don't worry" and "At least you're doing better than the Monster Raving Loony Party."

And finally to the spirit-sapping thing people always say to me when they are fresh out of positive spin and I am in the middle of some self-inflicted catastrofuck.

"Oh, well," they say with a snigger. "At least you might get a column out of it."

So here goes: In my humble opinion this is an invaluable primer for anyone—especially female—who thinks they would be great on the stump or hustings and a career in politics is for them. Or that it's easy to do center-ground politics differently, however "broken" the old politics is. It might answer, also, whether there is room in the center ground for a new political party at all (spoiler alert: no).

In July, two short months after our painful experiences in the polling booths, I bumped into my fellow Change UK candidate Stephen Dorrell. We agreed it would take "years of therapy" to process the trauma. We stood nursing glasses of summer rosé like *blessés de guerre,* limping survivors of some heroic disaster meeting for the first time to compare scars.

"Never in the field of political history," said the former health minister, his gaze logged onto a platter of hummus and flatbread, "has a party made so many mistakes in such a short time."

I can't boast that my "progress" was as Grand Guignol as the original rake's in Hogarth's satirical fable (having spent all his money on drink and whores, Tom Rakewell ends up an exhibit in Bedlam, where fancy Londoners come to laugh and point at him for their sport), but my little "walk with destiny" had its moments, as you will discover as you read on.

It's wrong to say, as Enoch Powell (not so fashionable now) once did, that all political careers end with failure.

Mine began with failure too.

Part Two

5

Exmoor

DAYS TO ELECTION   34

On Good Friday, I had arranged to be interviewed to be a prospective parliamentary candidate in an upstairs bedroom of our farmhouse in Somerset, deep in the Johnson pridelands, a hidden remote river valley dipped into the high heathery upturned bowl of the moor at the end of a two-mile rutted track.

When you get to the farm, there's no through road to anywhere. Just bracken-clad hills bulging from either side of the river like heaving bosoms, steep tangled cleeves, and glimpses of deer, kingfisher, badgers, and rare butterflies. Some guests arrive, get out of the car, look around, and go straight back again as they feel cooped in, and few teenagers find the lure of the high brown fritillary or a badger's set on a long walk (there's nothing else to do) can compete with the attraction of a London-bound car.

This place means more to me than any other and has been my "spiritual home" for fifty-three years.

As I waited for Skype to blip into life, I sat looking down the valley through the blue-bottled window frames to the visible sliver of the river Exe burbling and glittering in the sun. I kept my eye on the broadband strength on the top right-hand corner of the screen. The signal was flickering between one and two bars even after I'd ordered everyone in the house (everyone apart from Ivo . . . I was still keeping him in the dark) to turn Wi-Fi off on all devices.

The interview lasted twenty minutes, maybe thirty. On my screen I could just discern three fuzzy figures: Joan Ryan, MP, sitting in the middle—face a smiling sponge, voice a soft Lancastrian burr—but only half of each of the two men in suits on either side of her. As the signal and sound faded and stalled, I tried to convey my suitability and determination to defeat the foaming Faragists who had taken the Brexit Party to a commanding lead in the polls, coupled with deep knowledge and love of the West Country.

"I went to first school here in the village on the moor. Can you hear me okay?" I said.

"Yes, well, just, you sound as if you're underwater, but let's keep going," said Joan. Time was of the essence. They had had thirty-seven hundred applications and needed to find seventy suitable candidates in forty-eight hours.

"Okay, I'll speak up then," I said, hoping my voice wasn't carrying. "Er . . . my father was born in Penzance, while my grandfather was flying Hercules planes for the RAF when he was in Coastal Command in the war. . . . He crashed not once but twice in a two-week period of service," I shouted as if it were an achievement.

"Yes?" Ivo called from the foot of the stairs, thinking I was shouting for him. I ignored him. I was keeping the interview on the down low.

I didn't tell the selection panel, but after his crash Granddaddy had to stop flying, and that was why he became a farmer.

Johnson family group, Nethercote Farm, Exmoor, ca.1966, including Granny Butter (second from left), Granddaddy (holding Tiddles the terrier), Stanley (crouching), Alexander Boris (patting sheepdog), Charlotte (holding Rachel).

Granddaddy never spoke about the war, his DFC, or the fact that two of his crew died in the second crash. He had to wear one built-up orthopaedic brogue as his leg had been smashed on impact and was much shorter than the other one, and he'd also been very badly burned. He walked with a stick but still looked like John Wayne and would think nothing of wrestling a ram to the grass in the meadow. Sometimes he would have to crawl up the steep wooden stairs to bed on all fours. "His war wounds play up in this damp valley," Granny Butter would explain. She would watch him limp across the yard, and say, "I love that man."

"Er, and we've had a family hill sheep farm on Exmoor, from where I'm talking to you, since 1951," I continued, as all this went through my mind, forgetting to mention my trump card, even better than my grandfather's two prangs in two weeks:

I'd been expelled from Bryanston School in Dorset. (Everyone asks what for. I genuinely think it's because the staff found me annoying and this did for me far more than all my drinking, hitchhiking, smoking, making out with boys, and so on. I note that Lucian Freud was also expelled from Bryanston, so I am in good company.)

They asked me if I had any skeletons in my closet. Why I wanted to stand for the European Parliament. Whether I had ever broken the law.

"Goodness no, I am a tragic goody-goody," I lied. "I've never had so much as a speeding ticket," and trailed off, wondering if the points on my licence I'd been given for running a red light outside Buckingham Palace many years ago had expired.

Then they asked if I had any questions for them.

I cut to the chase. I asked them if they thought Change UK could win. A single seat. And they said yes. I did not know, then, one of the first rules of politics.

Never say you are going to lose. Even if you are.

I had—have—a lot to learn. That was Good Friday 2019.

The following day—Easter Saturday—one of the leaders of the Change UK party, Chris Leslie, MP, called me. I had never met him. I was in the middle of serving lunch (I had made what I call my Farmhouse Mummy soup, from stock simmered overnight in the bottom of the AGA out of two chicken carcasses, plus all the bone scrapings from plates, onion, and celery, potaged together with cabbage, swede, carrots, and—my mother's trick, this—a tin of baked beans). As I dished up, I saw his name flash on my phone. I let it go to voice mail.

Then a text chaser.

Hi Rachel, it's Chris Leslie here—could you give me a quick call? Cheers.

I got through lunch knowing full well what this portended.

A former shadow chancellor and joint leader of a national party—albeit a tiny baby start-up one with eleven MPs—would only be calling me in the middle of the Easter weekend to tell me one thing. That I was one of the several thousand who applied who had been selected.

I waited a decent interval until everyone had finished lunch and we'd cleared up.

Chris Leslie (nice voice like an old-fashioned high street bank manager) said he was "short-circuiting the usual formalities" as I had indicated in my panel interview the previous day that, if selected, I would need clearance from Sky News before I accepted any offer from Change UK. Leslie explained they wanted to put me top of the slate of six candidates for the South West, a vast constituency that stretches from Swindon to the Scilly Isles, including Gibraltar, former stronghold of the Lib Dems but now very Brexity in parts. Not only had I speedy-boarded my way onto their candidates' list; I was being asked to turn left into first class.

That was pleasing. I have been a girl from the West Country all my life: I went to first school in the village, I'd been to boarding school in Dorset, and the family farm with its drunken gates tied with baler twine, its vertical cleeves, its green hills dotted with sheep (mainly alive, but often dead) had been the balm to my soul since the day I was born. But I didn't live there full-time, and this mattered.

The day before, I'd been chatting with one of my father's two tenant farmers (the land is let for grazing). I'd been at first school with Robin and his brothers in Winsford. His cattle come into my yard to scratch themselves against my old Volvo and break into our barns in search of shade on hot summer days.

"Only down for the weekend as usual, Rachel?" Robin asked. "It's back to London now, I suppose?"

"No, I've been here the whole Easter week and am not leaving 'til after Easter Monday," I replied hotly.

Then I asked him when he was last in London. Robin was sitting on his quad bike on our track, rolling a cigarette. "London?" he said in his rolling West Country voice. "Never been."

I squeaked, "Never been to LONDON, Robin?"

Mind . . . blown!

He sucked at the end of his roll-up. "Never seen the need, Rachel."

. . .

AFTER THIS BRIEF CHAT WITH CHRIS LESLIE, IT DAWNED that I might be transitioning from journalist to politician. I had to at least warn my various bosses. I texted Toby Sculthorp and John Ryley, my editor and head of news at Sky, respectively. Apologetic as it was a Saturday, but urgent. Change UK had given me twenty-four hours to accept or decline their offer. I couldn't believe how quick it had been.

Compare my selection for the Euros, you see, with the Conservative Party's official system of candidate selection for general elections (bear with, as this long process takes a little telling).

First a keen thruster for Westminster has to apply and fill out a long form called "Application for Consideration as an Approved Candidate for the 2024 Parliament." There are vast empty spaces to fill in your extensive "political experience and campaigning activity" and "voluntary and community work" plus "other interests and memberships of groups, etc."

Confession: I once tried to fill in this form myself. It was in 2011 and after I'd met David Davis at a *Spectator* summer party and flirted with him. "Aren't you on the Conservative A-list yet?" he said, in a leading "I can make you a star" kind of way. "You should be!"

He gave me a number to ring. As I thought he was quite attractive for a Tory in his prizefighter way, I followed up. By return of post I got an application form. I even joined the local Conservative Party in Kensington before I filled it out, as evidence that I was prepared to go the extra mile. How naive I was. It asked me to list all the times I'd canvassed for MPs in my spare time, all the times I'd volunteered to help at the local association, manned the fête, and so on. It asked me lots of questions about all the times I had made a difference *politically.*

As I'd had three children under four while trying to hold down full-time jobs and had an ill husband who lost his job and had moved continents *en famille* twice, I felt that the Tories were perhaps missing a trick here. They were coming after people who'd already demonstrated a nerdy, Jacob Rees-Moggish devotion to the cause from the time they were in short trousers rather than normal people. I then hurled the application across the room and forgot about it.

Back to the form, though. After the usual education and employment sections, the applicant comes to Section 7, another huge fence to sail over without coming unseated: "Examples of challenges faced." This bit makes it seem as if the party were only interested in those who combine the survival skills of Bear Grylls with Sajid Javid's backstory. But Section 8 is even more daunting: "Your aspirations to be an MP and why you think you could make a significant contribution." And this is only the beginning of the process.

"If you pass that hurdle and are reasonably sane, you're invited to attend a selection day with the parliamentary assessment board," said a friend who has been through this procedure not once but twice and still not been selected. I had to double-check she said "sane" not "insane."

"There are eight of you, and these happen at locations all over the country. You're put through a battery of writing and speaking tests, and an hour-long interview where the person interviewing you doesn't have your CV in front of him or her, so you really have to sell yourself and impress them with your keenness. After that you're given a bunch of emails and have to order them in priority of importance, and draft answers to four, and then"—she shuddered to recall this part—"you have the Group Scenarios."

For Group Scenarios, candidates have to work in teams in tandem with another public servant, a councillor, say, or the MP from a neighbouring constituency, and react to some unforeseen event, such as a flood or a motorway bridge collapsing.

"They want to see how you function in a team and how forcefully you do your bit," she explained. "You also have to write a blog about being a new MP, draft a sample tweet, and pitch a private member's bill. After that, you go into another room and you are handed a piece of paper with a random subject on it and you have to talk about it for two minutes. You can't prepare."

"Gosh. And what was your subject?" I asked.

"Seaside towns and how to revive them," she said, as I wondered how clued up you would have to be to waffle on about coastal regeneration on demand.

If you make it onto the list, and Mustard really does have to be your middle name for this to happen, approved candidates receive the daily briefing—top lines from high command, and so on—plus notifications about seats that they can apply for. If they go for a seat, there's another form to fill, this one quite brief.

This one is only two pages of "why I would be such a marvellous local MP, pick me, pick me," so a comparative breeze. This is sent to a "sift committee" at Central Office, and then the local association checks through them, and around eight applicants are sent to hustings, out of whom three are chosen by executive members of the association. A final candidate emerges only after every local party member casts a vote.

It's a full-time job as far as I can see just making it through to the final round. The process is designed to weed out all but the most determined. I take my hat off to all concerned, especially as the chosen candidate then has to spend the next four years and tens of thousands of pounds often not being elected.

I put all this in to show that those who want to enter Parliament—or politics of any sort—have to demonstrate blanket commitment to the cause. They have to stick at it day in, day out, weekdays, weekends, bank holidays, tramping the streets, bearding passersby, fielding abuse, cold-calling constituents, canvassing, all on their own dime and in their own time. They are the crack troops of democracy.

For me, it took only one email on my iPhone and a twenty-minute interview on Skype to be selected (admittedly for a European plebiscite that nobody had ever cared about until 2018). I got off lightly.

When it came to Sky—my paid work—Toby Sculthorp rang back first. But he seemed far more interested in telling me about the hot new panellist he had signed for *The Pledge,* the debate show I appear on weekly on Sky News (9:00 p.m. Thursdays, Saturdays, and Sundays, in the unlikely event that you are interested). "We have another Rachel, a Corbynista younger than you," he said, as if that were what I'd been calling him about on a Saturday. "Rachel Shabi? She's very left wing, dark, and young," he repeated, as if I were already surplus to requirements, being middle-aged, liberal, and blond. "She writes for *The Guardian*. She's the exciting, new, dark, younger, replacement Rachel," he went on, without making any comment on my exciting news.

"Yes, but what about me being a candidate for Change UK?" I asked.

"What? Oh. Congratulations," he said. "I'll see you back on Sky in June, after you've lost."

John Ryley, the head of Sky News, was on a bike ride somewhere on the North Somerset coast. I told him that Toby Sculthorp had stood me down but had said he would have me back when I was no longer a prospective candidate for the Tiggers (nobody was used to calling them Change UK yet, let alone the multiple iterations that would follow). I repeated Toby's promise to have me back on the show to John Ryley in words of one syllable in case the bastard (Sculthorp, not Ryley) tried to sack me after the election and I needed a witness.

So: as of Easter Saturday, I no longer had any paid work, and was throwing my hat into the ring to fight a seat for a party unknown outside the Bubble to fight an election that was never meant to take place in an area that had largely voted to leave. I'd never stood for public office before. I found being a member of my garden committee in Notting Hill so vicious and time-consuming that I resigned after one term, drained by all the unpleasant rows about whether dogs should be on leads after dusk and whether to renew the play-bark under the slide and, if so, with what sort of play-bark. What could possibly go wrong?

Chris Leslie called.

"The campaign launch and reveal of the candidates is in Bristol this Tuesday, after Easter Monday," said Leslie. "I hope you can be there." It was April 20. I counted the days on my fingers. The Tuesday after Easter was St. George's Day, April 23—that is, in three days.

. . .

READER, WHAT DO YOU THINK MY FIRST THOUGHT WAS, after "I hope they don't want me to make a speech" and "What on earth have I done?" and "How will I break it to Ivo?"

It was this: What on earth will I do about my hair?

If asked, tell me a secret—it's that my hair is wavy and Farrah Fawcett flicky.

This is fine when you're on holiday, but if I go on telly without having it smoothed down, people go, "Does Rachel go to a '70s hairdresser?" or tweet pictures of me alongside Miss Fritton, the headmistress in *St. Trinian's* played by Rupert Everett, or Rick Parfitt of Status Quo. On Mumsnet there is even a thread called "Rachel Johnson's Hair" where users compare thoughts about my "look" in a somewhat competitive manner. One user wrote, "An Afghan hound with all those layers?" and underneath that: "No, a Seventies porn star."

I just put my name into Twitter (I know—it's a sign of madness), and a man called Benji Huish has tweeted, "I spend way too much time contemplating Rachel Johnson's fringe. Do hairdressers dare not touch it? Can she legally drive a car with it? Does it hide a dark secret? *Is it alive?*"

Given all this, how was I going to appear at the launch of a new center-ground party on Tuesday in Bristol without causing a Twitter pile-on about my hair? It was the Easter weekend and High Society, the nearest hair salon in Dulverton, eight miles away, was closed, as was Isis, the quaintly named beauty parlour next to Farthings ye olde farm shoppe. I couldn't leave the valley, as I had a house full of guests. There was only dog shampoo in the house. In terms of my barnet alone, I was doomed.

But first I had to break the news about applying, and being selected, to Ivo.

I asked him to meet me in the kitchen for a private word. I plunged into the long, narrow kitchen first, with its larder at one end and window at the other. He came in at my heels like a Labrador, and I gripped the AGA rail for strength and, indeed, warmth (Exmoor is always ten degrees colder than London).

His eyes widened, then narrowed, at my news. He hugged me, congratulated me, said all the right things in the right order, and it wasn't until later that evening when several bottles had been uncorked that out popped the cloven hoof. "They've only selected you for the publicity," my husband said, filling his glass with the £6.99 red from Sainsbury's.

It wasn't until the following week he let me have it.

"I have done years and years in Brussels, man and boy, I have worked there as a lobbyist," he ranted in his column in *The Lady,* making it clear that he had been far better prepared than I to have this greatness thrust upon him. "After all, I already know all the best restaurants—and bars" and "Why get the monkey when you can get the organ grinder?" and on and on.

Ivo moaned that my "blonde notoriety as the second evictee of *Celebrity Big Brother*" had somehow trumped his deep knowl-edge of the variable sheep-meat premium or the state aid regime as it applies to Liechtenstein. He had decided to gloss over the fact that I had lived and worked in Brussels too, and was not only the daughter of a Euro MP, but had actually worked in the European Parliament in Brussels in the late 1990s, which used to impress my children enormously when they came in to lunch at the excellent subsidised canteen or go up to my desk with its panoramic view of the Quartier Leopold.

"Mummy has a much bigger office than Daddy," they would say after lunchtime visits to the Paul-Henri Spaak building (I allowed them to believe that the entire edifice, including the hemicycle of the world's largest transnational parliament, was my private work space—so at least *they* thought I was important).

In spite of my husband's unequalled knowledge and patronage of the capital of Europe's watering holes, he did not catch the selectors' eye, and I did, but only, he made clear, because I was the sister of the man who had led Leave to victory. (I have long ago learned that you can't control what other people, even your husband of many years, think, write, or say about you.)

"Well done, Rake," said my brother Jo, when he came over to ours to borrow some ketchup, and shot out again in case he had to say something. He gave me a slightly pitying smile as if I didn't know what I had let myself in for and he was going to be the last one to tell me. I suspect becoming an MP/MEP is a bit like childbirth or marriage—that is, nobody would ever do it if those who had been there before them were honest about what it was really like.

Jo has been a fantastically successful MP for Orpington since 2010 (he tripled his predecessor's majority) and often sends me texts saying things like "Can't make tennis on Saturday after all—I've got to be in Biggin Hill." Or "Sorry Rake, it's the annual meeting of the Petts Wood Bowling Club Sunday—welcomes new members young and old, come on down—and I should be there, I'm afraid."

Anyway, after I told Ivo in the kitchen it became more real. I was in with a chance. A snowball's, but a chance nonetheless.

You don't vote for a candidate in the Euros. Instead, MEPs are elected using the closed party-list proportional representation deploying the D'Hondt method of distribution that only two people in the whole country understand; one of those is Andrew Adonis, and the other is Sir John Curtice.

I think I am right in saying that if Change UK managed to

win just a sixth of the vote in the South West region—roughly twenty-eight thousand square miles, four million voters—I would be elected. I would be returning to Brussels to live there for the third time in my life, only this time not as the "daughter of" a politician or *fonctionnaire* or the "wife of" a lobbyist or trailing spouse, or a "sister of" the first political rock-star celebrity, but as a public servant in my own right.

.   .   .

FROM THIS POINT, I LAUNCHED INTO MY SELF-DEPRECATING shtick with all speed. I told everyone it was bound to be hopeless but I was compelled to have a go. Above all, I didn't want anyone to think I would ever be self-important or anything but the unpompous "Blonde Show Pony" of my Twitter bio.

Still, I am a wildly overoptimistic person. I get this from my half-French grandmother, Granny Butter, and her son, my father, Stanley. I never think anything will go wrong. I never leave enough time to get from A to B as I assume there will be no traffic and I will never lose my passport at the makeup counter in Duty Free after my flight has been called. I almost always miss planes and trains as a result.

My father, Stanley, is so relentlessly positive that none of his six children have ever heard him say a negative word for as long as we have known him in his seventy-nine years on earth. If he really doesn't want to do something—and he likes to say yes to everything, from going into the jungle for ITV to climbing Kilimanjaro twice for charity in his seventies—he can only bear to say, "Could easily." (Tip: if a Johnson says "could easily" to anything, take it as a firm no.)

Now, my new party, Change UK, which had been sprung on the unsuspecting Bubble with much fanfare, tears, highly personal speeches, and smiley emoji on February 18, at one point polled 17 per cent. That was about twice as much as the Lib Dems, for comparison. Ch UK was currently bobbling around 9 per cent as the pending EU election period was upon us, but I needed only about 15 per cent plus to make it to Strasbourg for five years.

If you were a glass-half-full person, and I am a glass-completely-full person, there was a chance that once the campaign proper got under way, we could do a bit better than that, and I could be elected. But.

The Brexit Party had already stolen much of the available thunder by drip-feeding their "real people"–type candidates to Twitter. Every day or so an army major or a surgeon or a BAME CEO dropped. I would look at them on Twitter and think, "Well, I'd vote for them," as they seemed so normal. It was a clever strategy. It kept up interest in them, it kept the election in the news, and above all it worked because they looked like decent people you might have a pint with.

The Brexit Party thus produced a steady trickle of boldfaced-name candidates. One of these was also a "sister of"—Annunziata Rees-Mogg, a.k.a. ARM, the darling of the anti-European movement. Her adopted new Brexit Party was even further to the right than her birth party, the Tories, currently lashed to the hard-Brexit mast by the European Research Group led by Jacob Rees-Mogg, a.k.a. JRM, her own brother.

As her candidature was announced, ARM was pictured, pale and serious as an El Greco, swathed in a scarf and powder-blue jacket at the launch at a machine tool factory in the Midlands or somewhere. I checked her Twitter. She had fewer followers than me but more syllables to her name and her tweets were pretty punchy: the EU was a "sham"; people like me were "Remoaners." She came across as a brave and fearless Boudicca in her "fight to leave" the federalist prison Britain was in. There seemed to be any number of hills or ditches she would die on or in to "save democracy" and "change our politics for good."

I have no doubt that Annunziata is as delightful and courteous in person as her brother Jacob, but all this made me so depressed. When it came to the coming election, I knew that the Leavers had the best tunes. They sounded martial, propulsive, two fingers up to every establishment institution with an acronym. They were the daredevil outsiders against the smug featherbedded metropolitan elite who didn't know they were born. They couldn't make an economic argument for leaving the EU (remember Michael Gove saying, "Britain has had enough of experts"?), so they used an emotional one, which was far more effective.

Meanwhile, the Remain parties—and if you add Change UK to the Lib Dems, the Greens, Plaid Cymru, and the SNP—were all fighting over the same ground, with the same message, and splitting the vote between them.

Usually the Euro elections pass unnoticed in this country (the old joke is, if you knew the name of your local MEP, it meant you were the local MEP), but this one in May 2019 was already the most newsworthy in the four-decade-long period of the U.K.'s participation in that parliament's history. But it still seemed that a new center party's message was as easy to ignore by the travelling public as the safety briefing on board a BA flight to Edinburgh.

Change UK was boring on about tiny things, you know, like the future of the planet, the prospects of our children, and the health of the economy and the wealth of the nation, all of which were at risk if we dumped off trade on our doorstep, choked off immigration, and jumped into bed with a climate-change denier in the United States. But these compelling arguments had yet to cut through.

There were a couple of days to go until the launch in Bristol. I began to notice that my behaviour had undergone a transformation. I couldn't help it: everyone I met was a potential voter.

When I drove beyond Withypool to swim on the moor, I made sure I gave a polite wave to the motorist who had to mount a steep bank and mash his bumper into the bracken to allow my Volvo passage.

I worried about not going to church on Easter Sunday as I could pick off at least a dozen celebrants over sixty-five there in one go. I was paranoid that the publican in the Royal Oak was rude when I came in for a half of Exmoor Gold. What had I done? What had I said?

I began to understand why politicians spent their whole time going to rubber-chicken suppers and light-bite lunches and then tweeting out the gruesome evidence of their contact with their constituents: visibility is votability. As soon as you want to be called to serve the public, you have to be publicly servile and say things like "The people are my boss," just as the parliamentary website that publishes the records of Hansard for the U.K. is piously called TheyWorkForYou.com.

It was a whole new world.

.   .   .

LYNDON B. JOHNSON'S ONLY RULE OF POLITICS WAS YOU have to know how to count. I therefore counted my potential voters up before campaigning on the ground got going. In theory, I told myself, there were more than sixteen million politically homeless voters out there. Let's assume a good chunk of the four million voters in the South West voted Remain, in the university towns of Bristol, Bath, and Exeter and all the trendy crunchy-granola nut-clusters in the cereal packet like Totnes, Bruton, Stroud, and swaths of Wiltshire.

A million went to the People's Vote rally in March 2019, including me. More than six million signed the petition to revoke Article 50, including me. More than sixteen million voted Remain in the referendum, including me.

There were plenty of potential voters for Change UK out there, I reckoned, if we believed that the new divide in politics was extreme versus centrist, Leave versus Remain. I needed to hoover up at least a sixth of the total vote to win a seat, a seat that I would, if successful, retain for only six months, as the next hard stop in terms of our EU membership was then Hallowe'en: October 31, 2019.

The word "potential" was, I knew, doing all the heavy lifting in the above. We were a new party, in a pointless election, in a country fatigued by annual polls (the Scottish referendum in 2014, general election 2015, EU referendum 2016, general election 2017 . . .). I knew this would make everything even harder.

A vote is never owed. It is "earned." That's the nostrum, even though in many constituencies you could pin a red or blue rosette on a donkey and voters would vote for it anyway. But how was I going to even earn votes when nobody knew what Change UK was and what we stood for, and even if they did know, they suspected casting a ballot for us would be a wasted vote?

I didn't know then that my new entity's planning and organisation peaked back on Monday, February 18, when seven Labour MPs did this: they all wrote the same text on their phones, "I am resigning from the Labour Party," and pressed send at the same time (in another few days they were joined by another Labour backbencher and three Tories). From then on, it was downhill all the way.

.   .   .

AL RANG IN TO WISH ALL IN THE VALLEY A HAPPY EASTER. (We in fact use the formal salutation "Happy Eater" in tribute to the much-loved motorway café chain. Give me a Happy Eater over a Wild Bean Café any day.) He spoke to Dada, who was also in the valley and who also applied to stand as an MEP in these elections, but the Tories in their infinite wisdom had not selected him, despite his staunch service to the party man and boy, starting in the Conservative Research Department with Chris Patten in 1970.

Dada told him that we were all very well. "I said you in particular were perky but gave no further information," he revealed. I made a note to self: remember to tell Al I am standing on a platform of reversing the result of the referendum he led to victory. Before he reads it in the newspapers anyway.

On a walk, Jo made it clear that I needed to mug up, big-time. I needed to know which parts of the South West region had been Lib Dem, where the Brexit Party was strongest, and get a grip on the nuts and bolts: farming, tourism, manufacturing, services. "For example, is the South West a unitary authority?" Jo quizzed me.

Is it a what? I wanted to answer. I didn't let on that I didn't even know Bristol was a county until I looked up the "South West" on Wiki (Bristol is the capital of Bristol).

Chris Leslie called again, to make sure I was on board the bus. He said I was sworn to secrecy until the "reveal" of the candidates at the launch in Bristol. I tried to work out how many people I had already told. My family. Sky News. Oh GOD! My father! Then Leslie promised that my candidate info pack, details of the launch, and so on, would be with me shortly.

As soon as I gave my verbal assent to Leslie, it was all systems go—at the beginning anyway. Emails started filling my in-box, subject line "Party Launch." Every time I saw the two words

"Party Launch" together, my brain transposed them automatically to "Launch Party," as if I had been asked to a bunch of book launches in the coming weeks. That was, let's face it, far more likely for a middle-aged media tart (me) than embarking on a full-on election campaign.

Full disclosure: I had "parties" in my list of hobbies in *Who's Who* until I took it out as I thought it made me sound too superficial. Now I have to put country before party.

Over the Easter weekend, I also took calls from Joan Ryan, the MP who interviewed me, who was "just checking in." I even spoke to Anna Soubry—Soubs! She was in her greenhouse, she told me, sounding happy.

This was worrying.

I was clearly a big reveal at the launch; otherwise, why would the leaders all keep ringing, sounding so pleased I was on board?

If I'm the best they've got, I thought, we're already in serious trouble—before we've even started.

6

Bristol

DAYS TO ELECTION   30

The night before the party launch I washed my hair in the late Coco's old dog shampoo.

In the morning Ivo and I shut up the house and drove to Bristol, as I had a whole day ahead of me: rally, press conference, candidate briefing, and media training. That was the plan anyway.

We went in convoy. After almost three decades together, he knows from painful experience that any movement between A and B with me is a *Clockwise*-style test of nerves and therefore now prefers to move about solo and says he will "never make seventy" if we ever fly together again. Also, he was heading back to London before me.

On the phone the previous day, Chris Leslie had given me the heads-up that the *Evening Standard* had been handed the scoop on the slate of candidates and to expect a call from the political editor. On cue, as I was driving into Bristol, already lost, my phone started ringing. I hit speaker, and it was Joe Murphy, the political editor of the *Standard*. At that second I was driving into

The prospective European parliamentary candidate for the South West, Bristol, April 23, 2019.

the Millennium underground car park. A red neon sign flashed up as I drove down the ramp: "Car Park Full Delays Expected."

I was trapped between two cars, the occupants of which were no doubt happy to queue for hours before going to Fat Face, Caffè Nero, and White Stuff in the shopping precincts around. It was less than ten minutes to go until the official launch of the party.

I leapt out of the car, as Murphy asked questions like "How is the family taking it?" and "Have you told Boris yet?" and made begging gestures to the car behind me that was sandwiching me in to reverse out so I could leave and possibly dump the car at a bus stop.

"Where the fuck are you?" Ivo texted.

The driver agreed to reverse—I mentally worshipped him with my body—so I got back into the Volvo, shot out backwards, circled downtown Bristol a few more times, and finally parked in a multi-storey car park not too far away. Three minutes to spare until kickoff.

"Where the fuck ARE YOU???" Ivo texted again.

The launch venue was easy even for me to locate as it was in Millennium Square. The science and arts center glorying in the winsome name We the Curious was a vast glass box saying "We the Curious." Lots of people seemed to be headed in towards a mirrored disco ball the size of the Apollo space capsule outside the entrance. That was good. That meant I was not the last to arrive.

I received a WhatsApp from Sebastian Payne, the Whitehall editor of the *FT:* "Rumours here you are running for TIG."

Seb Payne is a friend. "Are you here in Bristol?" I texted back as I made my way into the building past some press photographers and tried to find the lift.

"Yes, staying around for the free pastries," he said.

On the third floor, hopefuls were milling in a large meeting room with sandwiches and cakes and croissants on a long trestle table, as if we were in the middle of the tea break of a village cricket match.

Outside was a large terrace where we spilled out, clutching our coffee cups, into the sunshine. It felt like the first day of a new school. My heart lifted when I saw the candidates for the South West numbers two, three, four, five, and six, and we signed our nomination papers. The slate could not be nicer. My number two was Jim Godfrey, who seemed vastly overqualified for almost everything, as this typical bio posted by Change UK proved:

Jim spent the last five years living and working in the US and since coming back has been shocked at how broken our politics has become.

With the Conservatives moving to the right and Labour to the left, Jim decided enough was enough. He wanted to be part of the solution—to mend our broken politics, help tackle climate change and work to bring our country back together again.

Jim is a certified leadership coach, start-up adviser and former senior executive at Starbucks, Jawbone and ITV. Prior to this he spent ten years in politics, serving as special adviser to the Secretary of State for Trade and Industry and director of communications for the Institute for Public Policy Research.

Jim is married with three children, lives in Bath and enjoys running up hills and playing the piano out and about in Bath at the weekends.

I paused at "running up hills."

Then there was Ollie Middleton, who looked much younger than my youngest child and had done more in his twenty-four years than me in my fifty-three:

Ollie Middleton is a former Labour parliamentary candidate, having stood in Bath at the age of eighteen in the 2015 general election, making him one of the youngest parliamentary candidates in recent history.

He later went on to run Liz Kendall's Labour leadership campaign in the south west. More recently, Ollie has been working as a political consultant, advising a range of large companies and organisations on a variety of policy issues. He is also studying for a Masters in Public Policy from UCL.

Number four on the slate was Liz Sewell, who was basically a saint who founded and runs an organisation helping women into work and is a former chief exec of Gingerbread, the lone-parent organisation, and number five was an old mate of mine called

Matthew Hooberman, who used to work for the Labour Party. According to his potted bio,

> He has a background in politics having worked for Gerald Kaufman MP, then shadow foreign secretary, from 1987–1992. He worked on both the 1987 and 1992 general election campaigns.
>
> Matthew resigned from the Labour Party in 2015, the day Jeremy Corbyn became the leader.
>
> He has worked in the US for the Institute for Policy Studies, Washington DC; and also in journalism and PR in London.

My slate, in other words, had been special advisers and parliamentary candidates and had spent years running either up hills or large corporations like Starbucks.

Last but not least was number six, Crispin Hunt, a dreamboat with Byronic hair and a vape never far from his delicate fingers who looked like a leftover from an 1980s boy band.

It turned out this was almost exactly what he was. According to a drooling piece in *The Guardian,* Crispin is "the 95-per-cent-cheekbone lead singer with Nineties cult rockers the Longpigs."

Crispin was no longer a hell-raiser but a Somersetshire family man and father of four, the chairman of the British Academy of Songwriters, Composers, and Authors, and a prolific hit maker for Ellie Goulding, Florence + the Machine, Lana Del Rey, Rod Stewart, and so on. Crispin was passionate, he told me, in his burning desire to "fight British populism with Britpop."

I couldn't help it, I loved them all immediately. They were experienced, clever, committed, and dedicated to our exciting new cause of "changing our broken politics." But given the polls, it was guaranteed that all our efforts would result in only one of us (me), or none of us, getting elected to the European Parliament. I was horribly aware that all our energy and efforts over the next four weeks, the travelling hither and yon on Great Western Rail, the hustings and the leafleting and whatever it was that candidates for election did, would be to shore up the moon shot that would see me touch down in Brussels, not them.

· · ·

NOTHING SEEMED TO HAPPEN FOR HOURS. THE HALL WAS filling with people and press and camera crews. We carried on eating pastries and exchanging pleasantries and WhatsApps with puzzled friends and press folk in the hall, waiting for something to happen. I hugged fellow candidates standing in their various regions, who had also been summoned to Bristol for the national launch, such as Gavin Esler, the former *Newsnight* presenter, and Annabel Mullin, the leader of the Renew Party, along with Jan Rostowski, the former deputy PM of Poland. I shook hands with the former health minister Stephen Dorrell.

Then, action: we were corralled into the anteroom containing the remains of the cricket tea and then made our entrance through the hall as flashbulbs popped, and sat on ranks of chairs onstage. I sat in the second row in order to hide from the cameras between Jan, the former fin-min of Poland, and my number two, Jim "running up hills" Godfrey.

Heidi Allen, MP, our "interim" leader, was first up, in a white T-shirt and cream jacket, with a dark shiny blow-dry I stared at with envy. She bounced on, curls bouncing, and gave her bouncy stump speech, in which she welcomed everyone, invited them to join the nine-week-old party, explained how both main parties had been hijacked by their extreme wings but it wasn't good enough to sit there shouting at the telly with a big glass of wine from the sofa; like her, we all had to DO SOMETHING!

Then it was time to introduce us, she purred. I felt my heart sink a little.

Heidi paused for dramatic effect to make sure she "had the room" and then went into full breakfast telly presenter mode to introduce the band.

"A call went out from Tigger Towers: 'We need a team!'" she gushed. "And wow, did you hear us! I'm very proud—like a proud Tigger mum!—to introduce our new Tiggers!"

When Heidi said "Tigger mum," I wanted to crawl on my hands and knees towards a fire exit and flee, but it was too late. I tried not to roll my eyes but practised my "our politics is broken" face.

Heidi introduced the candidates. I hadn't been asked to make a speech, even though Bristol was in my constituency, and I was lead candidate, so I was in danger of being asked. Instead, we had Gavin Esler. Heidi noted he had once interviewed Dolly Parton. "And as one of our candidates in London," she trumpeted, "he's going to be working more than *nine to five,* I can tell you!"

The familiar dark shape of Gavin took to the podium, his voice known to all *Newsnight* aficionados over fifty, vibrating with passion. "I think people are angry," he said. "I think people are disappointed. This is a great country. I am fed up with a few people on the far right dressed in flags claiming they are patriots. I want my patriotism back, and that will happen as soon as we get rid of Brexit and fix the problems facing our country."

Then a series of "normal people" (that is, not journalists and not former politicians from the Bubble) did the honours: a mumpreneur, and someone else I instantly forgot. I have reverse political skills: forgetting people immediately is chief among them.

Nick Watt, *Newsnight*'s political editor, was in the front row and had sat patiently through all this. When it came to questions, he was rat-up-a-drainpipe. "Why isn't Change UK in an anti-Brexit alliance with the other Remain parties? Your message is exactly the same as the Lib Dems," he said. It was clear this would be the clip the nation would be watching later on BBC Two. "Isn't this all a case of the People's Front of Judaea versus the Judaean People's Front?"

This was key and perceptive. We had a *Life of Brian* problem (why vote for us, not the Lib Dems, as we had pretty much the same message but there were more of them and they were a trusted brand?) that would pursue Change UK and scupper me in particular throughout the campaign. I could see the BBC and Sky crews crouching at the edges of the front row, and my husband sitting well to the back. It felt as though even he were avoiding my eye.

After the final closing speech from Chris Leslie, MP, suddenly this keen young man handed round large card placards with the Change UK logo—four horizontal stripes in various colours as well as the official black. We had to line up and wave them together for the cameras, like cheerleaders with pom-poms at a ball game. Some of us held them upside down. It looked as if we had no idea who we were or what we were for; the party was called Change UK, but our only policy was for nothing to change. I smiled for the cameras, but I could see the frozen expressions on the faces of the press pack feet away.

I did a short clip for Sky News (under orders from my Sky bosses). This was weird. I realised that I was no longer speaking for myself. I was speaking for a party, yet I had no idea what their policies were or what I should say. They'd only been a party for five minutes; they didn't have a manifesto or any policies, just some wishy-washy "set of values," but oh God, the camera was pointing at me and the red light was blinking and all I could remember from the website, apart from Change UK wanting a second referendum and for Remain to be on the ballot paper, was something about "evidence-based cross-party collaboration."

But nobody wanted to hear about that anyway. Nobody wanted to hear why I was standing for a new center-ground party. Or about our broken politics. They wanted to know about Boris.

"Does your brother know you're standing against him?" Sky's Kate McCann asked, as *The Telegraph* and the *Evening Standard* had already.

Suddenly all the cameras and journalists were clustering round, and mics were stretched towards my mouth, which was opening and closing like a dying carp.

"Erm, I'm sure that Boris understands why this is not a vote against Boris," I said, trying to push my way through them to the antechamber. "This is a vote for change. We need to move the dial. People need to have a say."

I tried to slide through the scrum onto the terrace.

Then I hid in a corner and pretended to be looking at the view in order to study my iPhone to see what Twitter thought of our launch. Instead, I saw that the Brexit Party had spiked our guns.

BOOM!

Ann Widdecombe was standing as a Brexit Party candidate and also for the South West.

If our launch was already a textbook example of how NOT to start a new party (two names, no policies, no logo on the ballot paper, eleven leaders, all the candidates revealed in one massive splurge), Nigel had played a blinder. He was announcing new candidates every day, to keep up momentum and dominate the conversation. He had a logo—a house on its side, roof pointing to the box on the ballot paper—a colour, hundreds of thousands of followers on Twitter, a grid with rallies, but above all he had a one-word party and a one-word message that nobody could fail to understand.

BREXIT.

I scrolled down on my phone. The timeline was full of politics around the European election the next month. Labour was also revealing its candidates: in the South West, I was up against Andrew Adonis for Labour and a bloke from UKIP, Carl Benjamin, who called himself the Sargon of Akkad, a YouTuber who was famous for only one thing: he couldn't decide whether he would rape Jess Phillips, MP, or not. I hoped I would never, ever be in the same room as him.

I scrolled down and thought, that's it then. Hey ho.

Widdecombe is an old dinosaur who thinks women shouldn't work, who demanded her own bathroom in the *Big Brother* house and got it, who is against gay marriage, homosexuality, and so on and so forth. Repulsive views, of course, but in these toxic times, Widdy is big box office.

For these were also views that are shared in private if not in public by a lot of over sixty-fives, not only in the West Country, but nationally, and I should know. I shared a bedroom with her for three weeks last year, when we both did *Celebrity Big Brother* for money. She made me and another woman on the show, Amanda Barrie, who was eighty-three, bring her biscuits in bed and wait on her hand and foot. Her "trenchant" (trying not to say "abhorrent," as I am polite to older women) views saw her almost winning the popularity contest reality TV show.

She was runner-up in *CBB* 2018. I was ejected second, which said it all really about the looming election.

Only former reality TV contestants were mad enough to fight it.

. . .

SEBASTIAN PAYNE FOUND ME, AND I FELL UPON HIM WITH relief as an emissary from a previous life. We have dinner at the Tory party conference, I was going to his wedding party, but as soon as we started chatting, a young man with hair *en brosse* and specs manifested by my side and pulled me away from my chum with some force. "Hold on. I'm talking to my friend Sebby from the *FT*!" I protested.

"Nobody is your friend," said the man, Malcolm Tucker–style (he turned out to be Chuka's comms guy—called Stuart—and was about the same age as my oldest son, Ludo. More of him later). "You are just copy now."

The candidates were herded back into the room for our briefing. We sat in rows in front of a lectern branded with the words "Politics Is Broken Let's Change It." A turbocharged chap called Harry Burns leapt onto the stage. (I asked him later, much later, where he got his energy from. "Drugs," he joked.) Apart from that, it was still like a school assembly at the beginning of term.

"Now, have you all signed your nomination papers?" Burns asked.

"Yes," we chorused.

"And have you handed them in?"

I made a mental note to change my Twitter bio from "Blonde Show Pony" to the far racier "Prospective Candidate for Change UK, South West and Gibraltar."

Beyond Harry, Bristol Cathedral slept on in the background, as yet unperturbed by the protesting yelps of all the Brendas from Bristol having to endure "not another one"—that is, another election they never signed up for.

Harry introduced the next speaker with these encouraging words as we embarked on our potential political "careers."

"Next you will hear from Peter. Peter is the man who will mean you don't go to prison," Harry said, and galloped offstage.

"My name is Peter Dunphy, and I joined Change UK on Wednesday," an older man in shirtsleeves then told us all.

"That's before most of us," shouted Stephen Dorrell, across the aisle from me. I glanced at him. He reminded me a bit of Gordon Brown. Same jowly, "stormy Heathcliff" type, late sixties.

Dunphy went through compliance, spending limits, expenses, what was an allowable expense and what was not, so complicated it was impossible to absorb, let alone remember. "How many of you have stood in a parliamentary election? EU election? Local council election?" he asked. A spatter of hands went up.

"Individuals won't be recipients of, or spenders of, campaign funds," he said, as if this explained everything. "All this will be done on a national basis; as we have only existed since Monday, we don't have a local party structure." He went on, "Meanwhile, all donations must come to the national party, not the regional groupings."

He told us to retain receipts either paper or digital, snapped on our phones, for accommodation, travel, and subsistence. This sounded hopeful to me. If we saved our receipts, presumably we would be refunded at some point?

He then talked about getting in funds, donations, the rules and caveats that applied here. Basically, potential donors could be foreign—that is, not British citizens—but must be on the electoral roll here to be able to fund candidates. Any donation above £1,500 had to be declared.

"Stick by these rules and you'll be fine," said Dunphy, explaining the limit for total spending for the entire electoral campaign, across the party, for everything, was £3.1 million. Then he added as an afterthought that it would be much more convenient if we didn't send in any receipts as it was a faff going through them, they were a skeleton operation, and there was no time or staff to do anything. We received this news in obedient silence.

I did wonder, if it was all such a scramble, why were we standing a full slate across the country rather than in two Remainy regions—London and the South East—and in alliance with the Lib Dems?

But there was no time for doubt.

"The whole system, the whole thing, is designed for elections in the nineteenth century, not the twenty-first," Dunphy said. "We are paying five grand per region, but we are having to get a bankers' draft for the South East, and the leaders are having to swear executive oath and will have to present a detailed breakdown of spend," he said. I think he meant that each region had a total budget of five grand, but then he said, "Basically, don't spend anything!"

Then he finished by saying donors (donors? What donors? I wondered) should be directed to the website, and then Harry Burns was back. "The campaign started today!" he said in a Harry Hotspur eve-of-battle way. "You guys are now candidates!"

He told us the three core messages that I wished I had known, say, before I had given a live interview to Sky News:

- Politics is broken, let's change it;
- We need a People's Vote for a final say;
- Brexit as promised can't be delivered.

There also seemed to be a fourth, which is that we needed to Remain and Reform. Everyone clapped. I forgot the key messages immediately. We were off to the races!

The next day, I was the splash—that is, front-page story—of two newspapers.

The *Evening Standard* had "Johnson to Stand Against Tories

(Not Boris—Sister Rachel Backs Remain Rivals)" and a picture of me with my mouth wide open arriving at a party at Tate Modern on the front page.

"Two-AGAs Johnson to Stand for Change UK," screamed the *Morning Star,* the only paper Jeremy Corbyn reads every morning, accompanied by a picture of me in a red dress also with my mouth wide open, like Munch's *Scream* (be in no doubt: all picture editors are sadists).

"Party slammed as flimsy establishment exercise as Allen and co. bring in Boris's super posh sister," ran the sub-deck. Most of Corbyn's inner circle are far posher and richer than any Johnson—we are "produce of many countries" like some cheap honey—but why let the facts get in the way of a good story?

The piece was priceless, saying *The Lady*—the weekly I once edited—was "favoured by aristocrats" (wrong—it is read by nannies and, increasingly, carers) and that Change UK was anti-establishment. It even quoted an appalling article I must have written at some point saying a house without a dog was not a home and that a house without an AGA was like a woman without a womb. "I'm afraid I have two Agas. Both are cream. I don't think I've ever disliked anyone who has an Aga," I was quoted as saying.

The next day I was sitting back in Notting Hill in a daze, thinking, *What have I done?* and I got this text from Gary Lineker.

"Is it true you've got a lovely pair of Agas?" he asked.

"Yes," I flirted back. "Revealed them both in Bristol City yesterday."

Tweet of the Day: Sebastian Payne of the *FT* tweeted a poll, asking, "Which 'celebrity' should be an MEP for the South West of England?" and listing all our names.

Thousands of his followers voted. The result was Widdy was

streaks ahead, on 44 per cent, while Andrew Adonis and I were tied together at 6 per cent, at the bottom, even behind Carl Benjamin, the man who joked that "there isn't enough beer in the world" to persuade him to rape a female MP.

Tweet of Day 2: Andrew Neil tweeted that the Change UK launch looked like "a low-energy sales conference in Solihull." I was thrilled by the Andrew Neil tweet. He had noticed us.

At least we were already annoying all the right people.

· · ·

WHEN I ARRIVED IN BRISTOL FOR THE LAUNCH IN MY PRE-tend professional-woman outfit of navy "blouse" and navy pin-striped trousers, I blended in okay. In fact, Joan Ryan, MP (the first Labour MP to jump ship to the Tiggers/Change UK), said, after I'd confessed to her about the dog shampoo, "Well, I think your coat looks very nice."

This is the thing about Change UK. Everyone is terribly nice to each other because they are doing politics differently, as opposed to tearing chunks out of people in their own parties. This is of course their Achilles' heel too, as nobody in the fledgling groupuscule wanted to be seen as pushy, domineering, and my-way-or-the-highway, with the result that Heidi was only "interim" leader and Chuka was only "spokesman" and every single decision was taken by a committee of eleven "collegiate grown-ups," which is no way of running a whelk stall, let alone a national political party that wants to "make a difference."

Anyway, if you are a woman after a certain age, the time, effort, and energy it takes not to frighten horses is truly terrifying. The female admin makes the grooming schedules of the Love Islanders—both male and female—look cursory and slapdash.

If you are seen in public and on telly (all MPs, policy wonks, hacks, bloggers, and so on are tapped up daily to do newspaper reviews, *Newsnight,* and *Daily Politics/Politics Live* as news has become showbiz, and producers are desperate to fill airtime with anyone who thinks everyone is entitled to their opinion), then you have to look tidy. Low maintenance does not survive contact with high-definition wide-screen TV for one second.

Tidy for men and tidy for women are different. Men are key-ready office suites; women are fixer-uppers. For a man, "tidy" means showering and putting on a suit and a tie. They don't even have to shave now as the stubbly metrosexual beard has become compulsory.

When someone asks me, "How's your week looking?" I don't think about deadlines or speeches or articles or appearances; my first thought is to go through a mental checklist of female-admin appointments beyond wardrobe and workouts (Victoria Beckham and Anna Wintour set the bar here: Posh treadmills for two hours a day; Anna Wintour plays an hour of tennis and has a blow-dry daily).

Men who prefer to think that we ladies wake up looking as glossy and gleaming as Melania Trump at a banquet during a state visit to the U.K., in a casual outfit, say, of a full-length, off-the-shoulder couture white gown, should probably look away now.

For women, especially presenters and MPs—and female MPs have to be screen ready at all times as there are cameras all over and outside Parliament—the following must be attended to on a daily, weekly, or monthly basis so that if a photographer snaps a picture or someone raises an iPhone at you on the tube, the results will not be at the very least career ending.

This is my grooming schedule, then . . .

Face: check nostrils and chin for horsehairs that have marched out overnight that you have to dig out with wire cutters.

Hair on head: check not too bushy or unruly.

Fingernails: must be clean and shaped and painted for TV.

Toenails (if seen in peep-toe shoes or sandals): must be summer ready and painted in a gay and currently fashionable colour that "pops," like neon orange.

Clothes: must be telly-friendly. If one goes on Sky, it is customary to wear what U.S. department stores call "career-wear": tight, colour-blocking body-con in dazzling primary brights, Hillary Clinton–style cream pantsuits, heels. The real Queens of Primetime—Kay Burley, Emily Maitlis, Laura Kuenssberg—also show their toned upper arms and shoulders, corded and rippling like Serena Williams after all the sessions they have slotted in with their personal trainer in their vanishingly small amount of spare time, and miles of thoroughbred bare legs.

There are various hacks to achieving this—that is, shortcuts. If I'm going on telly, I tell the lovely HMU (hair and makeup) ladies at the BBC and Sky to "ladle it on thick" so the paint job lasts at least two days. I also wash my hair before a TV appearance so HMU can give it a proper going over with a hot dryer and brush, so I can save the money I would have spent on a blow-dry.

Prep for my Sky show does clog the week, and when I say "prep," I don't mean mugging up on five topics from stop-and-search to the case for grammar schools, the reading up and researching on topics I know nothing about before I opine on them on national TV (the Nijinsky-like leap from total ignorance to complete authority is one all journalists have to perfect in order to survive five minutes in the trade).

No. The presentational challenges of television presenting

are . . . almost entirely presentational. This is because women may be prime-time when way past their prime in the United States, while here in Britain we are . . . just . . . not, and beating the clock has become a key part of the struggle for survival.

My grooming schedule is a brief morning mucking out of the stable compared with women like Kay who straddle the screens every day, for hours, rather than once or twice a week like me. For them, getting ready to go on telly is like painting the Forth Bridge. There is always a section that needs doing. Kay Burley has spent more hours live on-screen than anyone else, man or woman (that's what she says on her Twitter bio).

Here is her exclusive list you will only read here (and weep). Kay Burley's admin, then, in her own words:

Hair: blow-dry sadly daily in the morning for me unless I'm not working then it's scraped back out of the way. I also have monthly "deep root conditioning" so am in the hairdressers three hours at least. Drives me nuts but that's what happens when your hair is "without colour," i.e., grey.

Face: face mask every three days, every two weeks for facial, caci every six months, ultherapy every year and facelift—planning on every ten years. [You will have to Google "caci" and "ultherapy" yourselves just as I did.]

Nails: must be clean and shaped and painted for TV. My amazing housekeeper went on a course so I can have mine gel-painted at home.

Eyelashes/eyebrows: must be dyed and shaped. Not really something I worry about. I leave it to the makeup girls to tug on the odd rogue brow. Did try those individual eyelash thingies but it takes two to three hours every month—have to draw the line somewhere. So we use falsies instead.

Body: wax, then spray tan. Essential for my pale skin. Again, I got my amazing housekeeper to go on a course and we do it in a tent we set up in the kitchen.

Hair and makeup: used to take an hour. Now it's like those synchronised car-wash workers—I can be in, prepped by a production-line group of girls, and out the other end in twenty minutes.

Exercise: I also have regular podiatry because of the heels, reflexology to rebalance and exercise to keep the pounds at bay. Not sure how many of my male colleagues do the same . . .

I felt tired just reading Kay's schedule, and very jealous, I admit, of her housekeeper-beautician. All I've ever wanted!

I also asked Sky's political editor, Beth Rigby, about her grooming schedule (am beginning to sound as if I were investigating gangs in Rochdale), and she went, "Oh God."

Rigby left *The Times* for Sky and laments, "On newspapers all that matters is words on page; on telly it's lunch on teeth and dandruff on collar." In brief, she has a facial every month and an emergency eye mask for under-eye bags weekly. "I've spent hundreds of pounds on eye cream to try to get rid of them," she said, but we agreed that the only thing that worked is the most expensive beauty product in the world: sleep.

Beth has a "signature lip," a bright red slash of lipstick on her wide, mobile mouth. She runs ten kilometres twice a week, does Pilates once a week, and has an interval session with a trainer once a week.

"Men are two minutes in makeup," she says with a sigh. "If

I'm doing *All Out Politics* with Adam Boulton at 10:30 a.m. I have to rush, rush, rush to get the kids to school and myself into makeup before 10:00 a.m., but it's not as bad as it was before I was political editor. Then I had to get in at 5:00 a.m. for HMU, whereas my male colleagues could wander in casually at 5:45 a.m."

Newsnight's Emily Maitlis is lower maintenance and argues the female-admin hamster wheel is, in part, female vanity. "My hairdresser comes to the house as I don't trust anyone else to do it, so I arrive at the studio with my hair done," she says. "In the field [when she's out on a story or abroad] we can't spend hours prepping; ten minutes is all you need, and you're good to go."

Clare Balding always looks immaculate, but even she says she has to keep an eagle eye out. "I get warning texts from my wife, Alice, if I've got helmet hair."

Allegra Stratton left *The Guardian* for ITV via the BBC's *Newsnight*. She says, "I've never watched myself back doing a piece to camera and thought, 'I wish I looked messier.' " She says the rule of the makeup artists at ITV is that women can't look "distracting, mad, and over-bouffant."

When on the road or in the field, she does her own makeup and switches the camera on her iPhone to selfie to check it's gone on right. "It's all about brows and mouth for impact," she says. "If you're standing on a rainy high street doing a piece to camera and want to stand out, not oodles of foundation—that deadens your face." Even Stratton says things such as "red lipstick is my friend" and agrees that sadly there's no such thing as "too groomed" on TV.

This is not silly woman's mag stuff. When you do telly "as a woman," you know that people aren't really listening to what you say. They are inspecting you like a prize mare for defects.

Allegra Stratton says she gets "long texts" from her granny . . . about her makeup.

Michael Cockerell, the author of a book on TV and politics called *Live from Number 10,* says that going on TV is 90 per cent about appearance. His verdict on the Clinton-Trump leadership election? "It was bad luck for Hillary that she lost just when she finally got her hair right."

The hit novel of summer 2019, *Fleishman Is in Trouble,* put it well. At one point Rachel Fleishman, a top talent agent, is having a breakdown in New York in August. "Rachel looked at the other women, with their flatironed hair and their Botox and their fake tans. Why did they have to look this way? It was too much. There was too much being asked of all these women."

The sad truth is, I don't think men have any idea how much headspace all this takes up. How much is being asked of us, by ourselves, our jobs, and so on. It would terrify them. It terrifies me, anyway.

But it also puts women at a disadvantage daily.

This time-and-money-suck gap means that men have much more time and money to work or play than women on TV, who have to spend many hours a week and hundreds of pounds more than blokes . . . simply to do the same job.

Then, after all that time and effort, they still get binned off as soon as they hit fiftyish or so, as by that age they are practically a dodo in telly years, while the jowlier and paunchier and more antique their male rivals are, the more they are treasured by networks and the public alike. It's not fair, but it is what it is. Women have to rage, rage, against the dying of the studio lights far more than men do.

"I'm not going to let Mother Nature mug me off," Kay Burley told me.

. . .

MY VILE AND HEARTLESS OVERLORD AT SKY, TOBY SCUL-
thorp, once came into my dressing room and shut the door.
"What is it," I snapped, "are you going to fire me?" (I am always
being fired and then rehired by men who've forgotten they
sacked me five years ago; it's the circle of life in Fleet Street.) He
sat heavily in a black leather chair looking like Shrek in shades.

"I can't fire you," he said. "Unfortunately. One, you pretended to take your top off as a protest against Brexit on live TV
and the bosses loved it."

"Did they?" I squeaked. "Oh good—phew—what else did
they say?" I hoped to hear some positive reinforcements about
my contribution to the show's modest success from the network
high-ups. I wanted, I admit, some good feedback for once. But
Toby gave me a look to shut me up.

"I am still talking," he said. "Did I say you could start talking? Allow me to continue, please."

I put a sock in it.

"Two, you're too old," he said (he had his dark glasses on, so
I couldn't see his eyes to check whether he was being serious).
"I'd be done for ageism. Now get on with your work!"

7

Westminster

DAYS TO ELECTION   28

At the Bristol launch, each regional slate has been assigned an MP. The South West was lucky. We got the former GP Sarah Wollaston, MP for Totnes, chair of the very important liaison committee AND the health select committee and all-round good egg. The following week she called us all to a meeting in her Westminster office to work out "where to go from here."

I bumped into Crispin Hunt, my dreamboat former pop star number six as I was circling SW1, a bit lost in search of the Derby Gate to Norman Shaw North, a government building that overlooks the Thames. He was in black Levi's and navy linen jacket.

"Crispin!" I said, as he trailed his vape in his delicate musician's fingers, satchel around his shoulders.

We threaded our way back through Westminster (I had been going in towards the river rather than Whitehall) in lockstep and bumped into Kwasi Kwarteng, the undersecretary of state at the department for exiting the European Union, outside the Tesco Metro, next to the man handing out free copies of the

Standard. "Ah, the minister for Brexit," I greeted him. "How's that working out?"

Whenever I meet Kwasi, I can't help it. I remember what Amber Rudd had divulged at the Tory party conference in 2018 in Birmingham as we walked together to the *Spectator* party about the full extent of her former squeeze's . . . manliness.

I contemplated Kwasi as we stood there, tourists and spads in suits with lanyards dodging around us, Amber's words still sounding in my ears. I kept my eyes trained level with his stained tie.

Norman Shaw North, where Sarah's office was, is part of the Victorian former HQ of the Met. It is a handsome, looming edifice made of banded red brick and white stone, bang next to the Red Lion pub. Sarah Wollaston came down to let us in and go through the usual airport-style security of the parliamentary estate. She was beaming. It was as if all Change UK MPs had been told to smile at all times, to prove their principled defections from their parties had cheered them up no end and if only others could follow the eleven Pied Pipers, they too would see the light. In Sarah's case, her ease and cheerfulness seemed natural, and we followed her up the plush red carpeted stairs.

Sarah is reassuring and motherly in every way, broad in hip and beam, and I felt safe and protected for the first time since I'd "entered politics." Sarah was a GP. She was our den mother for the South West slate. Whatever happened, however awful, Frau Doktor Sarah would take care of us.

The place felt like a cross between a minor public school and a dignified care home somewhere hushed like Edinburgh: deep pile carpet, busy wallpaper, and the names of MPs on the doors. Wollaston was on the second floor, next to the Right Honourable Priti Patel (now hard-line home secretary who Twitter always whines wants to bring back hanging but was always naughty charm itself, a tiny Tory Tinkerbell, whenever I meet her).

"Gosh," we all said when Wollaston unlocked and we filed into her office.

It was a vast corner affair: DHS sofa nook in a bay window, for meetings, the other side homely, decorated with poll boxes saying "Salcombe," gay nautical bunting, posters, and a messy desk.

We sat at a big dining table, with a coffee machine on a side table next to us. We Skyped in Liz Sewell and Matthew Hooberman, the two members of the slate who couldn't make the first campaign meeting. Matt's only contribution came at the end, when he announced that thanks to dodgy broadband in Bruton he could hear only one word in three.

"Wow," we all went, again, while the coffees and teas were made.

"Yes," agreed Sarah. "Bob Stewart charged in here to measure the curtains after I left the Conservatives as he thought he could kick me out."

"Ah, Bonking Bob," I interjected, as I saw the capacious couches again in a new light. (I only said "Bonking Bob" as that is for some reason the affectionate nickname given to Colonel Bob Stewart, MP for Beckenham, across Westminster and the tabloids.) "I bet he did!"

"Indeed," Sarah continued. "He didn't think I was entitled to keep the office as I wasn't a Tory anymore, but as you can see, I've hung on. Theresa May let me keep it as I chair the Liaison and Health and Social Care Committee." (Note: Life comes at you fast. Sarah Wollaston hung on only until August, when she was summarily evicted by the new PM's assistant chief whip.)

We then tried to work out next steps.

Basically, there was no ground operation, no leaflets (yet) to distribute, and no policies apart from #brexitshambles and #putittothepeople, and we had less than a month to cut through with our message: referendum, remain, reform, and after that we wanted to deliver evidence-based policies beyond Brexit.

Ollie Middleton, the Milkybar Kid look-alike youngster of the slate, said we needed a manager. Right away. As it happened, he said, he knew just the person: Jo McCarron. She'd stood as a Labour candidate too. But we needed to pay her. Especially as her husband had buggered off, and she was single mothering outside Bristol.

We all agreed that Jo sounded just the ticket, but Sarah Wollaston looked worried. I did not know why then.

This was because Sarah knew.

Her takeaway from the preelection briefing at the launch in Bristol was that we had to keep receipts, but this was a mere accounting exercise. We would not be reimbursed. She promised she would check, but this, she intimated, was her understanding.

The good news was that each regional slate would have a fighting fund of £3,000—out of the total of £5,000 per region—to cover all of us for the whole campaign. At Ollie's suggestion we immediately allocated Jo McCarron (whom only Ollie had ever met) two-thirds—that is, £2,000—of our entire budget.

It seemed the right thing to do at the time.

I knocked on Priti Patel's door when I nipped to the ladies (miles and miles away, as is compulsory on the estate, famous for having no washbasins in the Lords for centuries), but there was no answer.

I came home and collapsed on the sofa and watched Man U versus Man City and ate curry that Ivo had made from scratch.

"I have two parents who changed careers," my son Oliver announced as we ate. "One's become a politician and the other's become a chef."

· · ·

ON MY DAUGHTER'S TWENTY-FIFTH BIRTHDAY ON APRIL 25, I played tennis with Johnny Hornby. Johnny is the top adman whose agency, The&Partnership, was working pro bono for Change UK and was even giving the party free office space in Soho. The third player was Russell Chambers, also a mate, who by coincidence was drumming up funds for them, which was as good an example as any of nominative determinism. (What do you call a man who is whistling up money from donors for a box-fresh-new center party? You guessed! "Rustle.")

As we played, we agreed that so far the branding was shit (four horizontal black lines), the name was shit (Change UK— the Independent Group), the fact we didn't have a leader was shit, and the fact that we were polling less than a third of the Brexit Party—around 4 per cent or so—was totally shit. But still. I am very much a glass-full person and so, bizarrely, is the creator of this catastrofuck, the former prime minister David Cameron, who also happens to be one of my current tennis partners and was the fourth player that day. After the traditional two sets, we have coffee on the terrace and indulge in what he calls some light "Brexit therapy." He says all the above are essential to maintain his mental health. (I know. Please don't write in or @ me or send death threats!)

"So where are you on the list?" DC asked as we tried to win the first set. I was keeping a note of all the swearwords he used when he muffed a shot, which had an escalating sequence of intensity, so the easily offended should look away now.

If he double faults, he hisses, "Big blouse, David!" Or, "Fat bugger, you could have made that, David!" Then the c-word, followed by "fat c*nt" or "lazy fat c*nt" or "shit the bed." Strangely, if he misses a total sitter and he is really, really cross with himself, he will say, in a reflective voice of purest calm, "That, David, was the worst shot in lawn tennis."

Despite his potty mouth, he says the six scariest words of the English language are "Theresa May called for a chat." Full disclosure: he has very blue eyes that talk, and smooth, tanned skin with the expensive sheen of health. He might have destroyed the country, but I can't help liking him.

Ah, where was I on the list? David Cameron had enquired.

"I'm first on the list," I answered, trying not to let a note of puffed pride enter my voice. Then I put my return of serve into the net. When we're behind, David always announces the score out loud—love thirty, love forty—in a meaningful way as if to remind me I've lost us the point and ought to pull my socks up.

"Really? First?" he said, thwacking a ball into the far corner. A winner. "You'd better watch out; you could be in Strasbourg for the next five years."

I laughed. During the next point, DC shouted, "Kill!," which is what he always says when I am up at the net and there is a sitter to put away. If I miss it, he says, "You need more horse ketamine."

As we changed ends, he asked, "Have you looked into the salary and expenses of being an MEP?" I hadn't. I really hadn't. This wasn't about the money. And I didn't expect to win. DC told me that after the nightmare of the MPs' expenses he'd looked into MEPs' allowances, as he suspected that would be the next political PR disaster coming down the pike.

"You know what? MEPs get 4,000 euros' spending money a month on top of their salary," he said. "And six-figure relocation costs." He smashed a return of serve. "I'm in the wrong place, I said to myself!" (The PM's salary is £150,402 a year.)

After the game—as usual we won the first set and lost the second ("Just like the Tories," DC said, "we veer between complacency and panic"), we had eggs and coffee and our usual spot of Brexit therapy.

During this session, DC thought (back then, that is, April 2019) that when it got to the hard stop of Hallowe'en, after which we had to leave deal or no deal, do or die in ditch, there would be another extension. It would be Hotel California. Brexit was not an event; it was a process and could be made to go on for ever and ever. He spoke as if Brexit would see all of us out, and our descendants in a hundred years would still be arguing for Revoke while the great-great-grandson of Steve Bray, the man in the "Ode to Joy" hat who bellows "Stop Brexit" on College Green, would be wrapped in the EU flag for SODEM (Stand of Defiance European Movement) every day outside Parliament, 9:00 a.m.–6:00 p.m.

Well. David Cameron was not wrong about everything.

"I am resigned to the Johnson ascendancy," he told us on the terrace. "There's no stopping your brother now." And then he said that the only reason my bro had supported Brexit (and then TM's deal, once) was that he wanted to be PM.

I didn't argue. Whatever I say gets me into trouble, and I did not feel it was the place to argue the toss in public with Cameron about why my brother wanted to become PM, as it is the sort of conversation that other members pay to come to the tennis club to avoid.

· · ·

LATER I CALLED TOM BALDWIN, ED MILIBAND'S FORMER spokesman, who was now running the People's Vote campaign group with Alastair Campbell, the punchy former press secretary for Tony Blair. I'd last spoken to Tom when I was in Jamaica. He and James Chapman, a former political editor of the *Daily Mail,* had booked me for a conference call that I had taken on a sunny terrace. I munched away on my breakfast mango as they tried to persuade me to write an open letter to my brother arguing that the only way to avoid the country committing economic suicide was to put it to the people and have it published in the *Daily Mail*. I'd refused. It was increasingly clear to me that my only use to editors, broadcasters, campaigners, lobbyists, and Remainers was to get me in the papers as being disloyal and oppositional to my own beloved brother and create unfortunate (for him) headlines. My only utility was disloyalty.

After I'd declined to write the open letter, I was not in credit with the People's Vote lot, even though I'd launched Women for a People's Vote on my birthday in 2018, at the Royal College of Nursing, along with Alastair's daughter, Grace Campbell, the campaigner Caroline Criado Perez, and sundry feminist luminaries.

Tom Baldwin was polite but distant when I rang to see what we could do, Change UK plus People's Vote, together. He explained in a weary voice that the People's Vote didn't and couldn't align with any political party. Ah.

That was not quite the whole story.

I didn't know then how toxic the arch-Blairite Chuka was to Old Labour or that Jeremy Corbyn refused to be in the same room as him. I hadn't worked it out (am sometimes a bit dim) that People's Vote was run by two dyed-in-the-wool reds, Campbell and Baldwin, who couldn't help not wanting to stick the boot in Labour's EU-neutral policy of sitting on the fence for as long as they could. Anyway, I got the sense that Best for Britain and the People's Vote lot were not exactly against us, but we were not helping the cause.

In fact, all the different Remain lobbies and groupuscules were ferrets in a sack. They couldn't work together, despite everyone wanting the same thing, and allowed the vanity of small differences (for example, did they want a second vote, Revoke, or remain-and-reform?) to undermine them fatally just when the country needed them most.

Still, People's Vote produced tons of useful data and information proving that leaving the EU is a country declaring economic war on itself for the first time. The outfit called Best for Britain also produced good research as well as data mining and a tool that plotted the polling of each party in each region. According to this helpful algorithm, it was forecast that the Brexit Party would win two seats in the South West, Labour two, Lib Dems one, Tories one. And Change UK . . . none. Zero. Zip.

What the tool told us in late April was this.

Every vote for Change UK was effectively a vote for the Tories and the Nigel Party—as it was a vote missed for the Lib Dems, the Greens, or any other pro-Remain party that might be in with a chance. No wonder everyone hated us—especially Remainers—before we'd fought a single seat.

· · ·

I SPENT THE REST OF THE DAY GLUED TO MY PHONE. THIS was normal. I seem to spend hours reading Change UK threads that don't concern me at all. ("Just arrived at the car park," someone called Sophia B will post, along with a photo of a car park somewhere in her region. "Are we meeting at a coffee shop?" Someone else attending the York rally will tell around 140 people in the WhatsApp group, including busy MPs, "Upstairs in Patisserie Valerie opposite Jorvik Centre. Please let me have your coffee orders!")

A note on WhatsApp: This is where politics actually happens. This is where the events, the grid, the PR strategy, the lines to take, the launches, the plans, are all placed first, which means my screen time per day will go from about three hours to eight hours. I could literally print the WhatsApp group as a book as it tells you all you need to know about the logistics and seat-of-the-pants, *Blue Peter*–style, sticky-back-plastic effort of launching a party from scratch as a pop-up to fight an election in less than a month.

My new life was ruled—on WhatsApp—by a sweet woman in her twenties called Elle Dormer. "I'm a refugee from Tory Central Office, but we don't talk about that," she said. Elle was in charge of press for the MEP Change UK candidates.

The entire day disappeared just managing and responding to bids: radio, TV, print, and, increasingly, podcasts. Yes, podcasts. They are, I'm afraid, just like opinions and arseholes (everyone has one) and are yet another platform on which to come a cropper.

I had to ignore repeated orders via WhatsApp to "push" social media posts on Instagram, Facebook, and Twitter. This was problematic. With the best will in the world, I couldn't honestly be expected to tweet things like "Huge support is building across the country with packed rallies in Nottingham and Norwich" or videos from #Women4Europe, #WomenAgainstBrexit, and #W4PeoplesVote.

I felt bad about it—but not that bad. I had my followers to think of.

In fact I said no to all of them apart from one: the *Chopper's Brexit Podcast*. The family of Chopper—that is, *The Telegraph*'s chief political correspondent, Christopher Hope—was in a terrible bus accident in which his daughter lost a leg, and I am a terrible softie. I was also tempted by "White" Rod Liddle's offer because he made me laugh when he described the Extinction Rebellion as "berserk menopausal women in tie-dye" doing interpretative dance in front of the pink boat at Oxford Circus.

And Matt Chorley of *The Times* and Simon Walters of the *Daily Mail* both called with the same brilliant unusual and original idea that they told me I wouldn't be able to resist. They wanted to interview me and Annunziata Rees-Mogg together as a sort of Sister Act.

Declined!

· · ·

JO MCCARRON, THE SINGLE MUM IN BRISTOL RECOMMENDED by young Ollie, duly hopped on board as the slate's paid organiser. Our South West WhatsApp group thrummed and buzzed about meetings, rendezvous, but most of all leaflets. Where were they? Would they be printed in time for our Change UK stalls (outside a supermarket in Bath on Saturday and outside a supermarket in Bristol on Sunday, so it was shaping up to be a fun weekend)? We had to set up a Facebook page for our group and a YouTube channel.

Unlike the Lib Dems, you see, we did not have a "ground game" (it is easy to slip into Westminster dialect), nor could we, given the size of the constituency. As far as I could see, there was no earthly point in my trying to knock on doors and beard poor horrified Brendas to badger them to vote for us in the European elections to endorse our one policy, which was they should vote yet again in a second referendum. People were fed up with voting, and they were fed up with Brexit.

This could only be an air/digital war, to be waged via interviews on TV, radio, and across "social," as well as live events like hustings and rallies. Given the interest in the lineup in the South West (me, the Sargon of Akkad, Ann Widdecombe, Lord Adonis, and Molly Scott Cato, the Green MEP), the dozens of live debates would be attended by media on the lookout for pratfalls and gotcha moments. As a prolific media tart, I assumed

I was best deployed as artillery in the air war in town rather than as a foot soldier on the ground.

Yet everyone I met in London raised an eyebrow at my presence in the capital. "Aren't you canvassing in your constituency, ha-ha?" they would ask, as if I should be personally shaking the hand or leafleting every constituent from Swindon to the Scilly Isles and should be out on the stump simply to prove a point. At the outset of the exercise I felt sure we couldn't and shouldn't run a modern twenty-first-century campaign like a Victorian by-election. This was—it had to be—a virtual election.

Which was why, as night follows day, I spent the next three weeks in farmers' markets and Sainsbury's car parks in the cathedral towns of the West Country, bed blocking potential voters as they tried to go about their daily business. There was no alternative. When the adrenaline of electioneering hits the endocrine system, you're hooked. It's like a shoot-'em-up video game. You all have the same amount of money and time, and the winner is the one with the most votes at the end.

You flick onto Twitter and see that Andrew Adonis is at a technical college in Bath or that Ann Widdecombe is in—I am not making this up—Widecombe in the Moor. Having seen that, you can't just sit at home in London because you've got to be in Millbank for the *Daily Politics* on Wednesday. You have to get out there and rack up your kills—even if the polls are saying it's game over already.

8

Bristol

DAYS TO ELECTION   26

Before heading to Sarah Wollaston's seat of Totnes to campaign in the crunchy gluten-and-single-use-plastic-free granola capital of the South West, I had to do a quick day trip to Bristol. On the train, I tried to upload a video of me-on-the-train to my Instagram account. I honestly didn't see the point. This was before Rory Stewart did his Rory Walks *en marche* walkabouts and broke the internet with all his extempore from-the-heart handheld pieces to camera in the Tory leadership campaign.

I had to go to Bristol because I was the lead candidate, and our team manager Jo McCarron's brother Tim was all set up to make videos of the slate on the stump to release on our Twitter and Instagram feeds. Yup. I was going to Bristol and back on a Sunday (in politics there is no such thing as a free weekend) to appear in a social media clip.

I couldn't grumble. One, three others on the slate were doing it too. Two, politicians are expected to do this stuff all the time to "connect with" the voters, and to show their constituents or prospective constituents they are there, which is why MPs' social

Family out on the stump campaigning in London for Boris's reelection as mayor of London, 2012. *Left to right:* Leo, Rachel, Boris, Stanley, Jo.

media feeds swell with images of them out and about, declaring themselves thrilled and proud to be opening a garden center or attending a family fun day out, Rotary Club hog roast, or charity event. It's a way of virtue signalling and buttering up your base at the same time. But it's all a bit tree falling in the forest. If you open a garden center in your constituency, but you don't post a picture of yourself opening the garden center, can anyone be sure it actually happened?

Despite coming from a very public, annoying, large family, I find doing anything straight and sincere squirm-making. Jokes, yes. Passionate intensity—please, God, no. Not in my name! I was not sure this was my comfort zone. According to my family, at least, I don't like meeting "real people." My children accuse me of glazing over when even "loved ones" are speaking. They often say they ask me questions and I don't answer. (When accused, I tell them, "I answered in my head"—doesn't everyone?)

I always forget a face and a name. I am constantly getting "we've met several times, the last time was at the Strawberry Fayre in Henley in 2008, who am I, I bet you don't know, do you?" when I can't even remember my husband's birthday most years and we have forgotten our wedding anniversary every single year except one, and that was only because my own mother rang in the morning on the day to remind me.

This chronic lack of user-friendliness is why I was kicked out of the *Big Brother* house in 2018 after nineteen days. Wayne Sleep was telling me about his time in the jungle in *I'm a Celebrity*. I zoned out and wandered away in mid-sentence. My husband and children were watching me from the sofa at home and told me they all chorused, "That is so Mum."

On the train, I uploaded the pointless little video to my Instagram and then sent out a boring tweet about "how much I was looking forward to getting back to Bristol" to meet people in the Watershed. It had twenty RTs, which was respectable.

From the station, I walked to the Change UK stall in the Watershed, which was trusty Liz Sewell with a camping table, a small whiteboard, and stickers, our manager, Jo McCarron, and her brother. Liz was asking passersby whether they supported a People's Vote and sticking their stickers in two columns, headed "YES" and "NO" in red marker pen. Like the Ancient Mariner we stoppeth-ed around one in three.

Lots said they wanted another vote, but those who did had the distinct tang of climate-change activists about them (tie-dyed clothes, white dreadlocks, Birkenstocks). They were mainly intent on vegan street food and probably only agreed about wanting another vote to make us go away so they could get in the queue for spicy bean tortillas. We felt very excited when we put a yes sticker up anyway.

The crew off a Dutch sailboat stopped to chat. Two handsome rugged beardies in navy Musto waterproofs and technical trousers were wandering round the Watershed, like everyone else, on a Sunday afternoon. I was definitely prepared to give them the time of day, so detained them. After doing a sail around the coast, they were now moored in Bristol harbour, they told me in perfect unaccented English. They were crewing for a wealthy man who had planned to leave the Netherlands on March 29 and invade Britain, they explained.

"That sounds fun, but why invade Britain?" I asked.

"Because after Brexit you would be so weak as a country," the taller of the Dutchmen said. "We can take you over. But Britain didn't leave on March 29, and we came anyway."

I agreed with them that there was always a certain merit in sticking to plan.

Such a pity they couldn't vote for Change UK, but at least the Dutch sailors were on board: they lamented the popularity of Geert Wilders (that's the awful thing about populism—it's popular) and how awful it would be if the Euro Parliament was filled with far-right Ukippers or Brexiteers like Nigel Farage, who just came to Brussels to insult the MEPs and the institutions. "There are many in the Netherlands who want to leave the EU too," the weather-beaten pair told me, as I admired their strong brown hands, "we could have our Nexit too."

I reassured them about contagion. So far, the fact that it had taken the U.K. three years not to leave and tie itself in knots had had, we agreed, the opposite effect. The EU was more united than ever.

"You won't have Nexit if people see how difficult it's been for the U.K.," I pointed out. "The reason we haven't left is not because people are being bloody-minded, although it was ironic that the people who have been blocking Brexit in Parliament are the ones who are supposed to want it most. The reason we haven't left is because it's like trying to remove the fresh eggs from a baked cake." (I use this line a lot. It has what is called "cut through.")

In Bristol, that first day "on the stump" confirmed two things.

The average punter is far more well briefed and clued up than you think. The ones who do stop and chat have their bullshit detector turned up to eleven. As soon as you get "out there," you realise the point of leaving the Bubble and starting to widen your circle beyond, say, Sebastian Payne of the *FT,* Adam Boulton of Sky, or Rachel Sylvester of *The Times.* In fact, I found out one thing pretty fast: many of the people I talked to were not thinking what I was thinking at all.

What they were thinking was, get on with it. The people have spoken, you lost, get over it. In the unlikely event of a second referendum, the Remain alliance's only hope against the thudding force of the Leave campaign's "Tell Them Again" slogan or the Tory party's "Get Brexit Done" would be to call the further plebiscite a "People's Verdict" with the campaign slogan "Make It Stop."

Thick of It Moment 1: I managed to tag the parody account for the South West group, not our official Twitter group, in my first tweet. I suppose I should be pleased that there WAS a parody account for us so soon. It felt like a compliment.

Thick of It Moment 2: The leaflets weren't ready for the stall, so we just handed out photocopied A4 pages of our logo and took people's names and emails so we could hound them mercilessly.

Thick of It Moments 3, 4, 5: Our only policy was to stop Brexit (the Monster Raving Loony Party had more policies than we did, even if they included introducing a 99p coin and painting Big Ben with polka dots). But the Lib Dems had registered the slogan Liberal Democrats Stop Brexit Party on the ballot paper, thus making it look as if they, not us, were the alternative to Farage's Brexit Party.

An activist had already resigned and whinged in *The Times* that the candidates' list was packed with placemen and not enough "gender balance" (I assume that means women, but God knows these days) and the only boldfaced names were media retreads and "D-list public figures." (I was flattered. But that's no way to talk about Gavin Esler!)

Ping! WhatsApp. A poll. Our numbers since I joined had dipped from 9 per cent to 6 per cent.

My heart sank.

·   ·   ·

I REACHED OUT IN PANIC AFTER THIS POLL TO BOTH SARAH Wollaston and Chris Leslie, but they both laughed and told me not to panic.

I was amazed by the composure of the leadership in the face of the polls and the media narrative that had already been established that we had flubbed things at every turn. But then, I had not yet learned that politics is the art of putting on a brave face and saying things like "the only way is up" and "in politics you have to believe that however bad things are, someone, somewhere, is having an even shittier day than you."

Meanwhile, the media offers kept rolling in. *Panorama* had bid to follow me around for a documentary. Elle the press person was not keen. Camilla Long, TV critic of *The Sunday Times,* agreed. "Sounds like a stitch-up to me." I dug deeper and found out that the editor also wanted to follow around Ann Widdecombe "for balance," as we were in an election period. So that was a no then.

Ping! My WhatsApp. Another poll! Lib Dems were on 11 per cent and Greens on 6 per cent and Change UK was on 3. Our poll numbers were in free fall. From 17 per cent to 9 per cent to 6 per cent and now 3 per cent after the launch. By polling day we could be wiped out completely.

I felt it was my fault.

I was beginning to hope that people thought Change UK was a Brexit party and voted for us instead. I was amazed by how seasoned campaigners like Sarah, Chuka, and Chris took the tide of bad news on the chin and kept their gaze on the horizon. It's as if they knew that it wasn't going to pan out, but it wasn't for me—a political newbie—to point out that the struggle naught availeth.

We had to fight on; we had to fight on to lose.

9

Totnes

We convened at the farmers' market in Totnes on the first Friday in May.

I left the Volvo on the high street and ran up, late, having driven across from Exmoor. The team had set up the special camping table by a fancy coffee shop called Brioche in an arcade. I had never been to Totnes before, but despite the cold I was charmed; it was like going "back to the garden," as in Joni Mitchell's "Woodstock."

Rather than leaflet hoary hippies with their "The EU is my bag"–branded hessian carriers, all I wanted to do was putter about the bustling stalls selling organic cotton, "leather" accessories made of reclaimed inner tyres, Peruvian hats, and vegan baked goods and browse for vintage blue-and-white-striped Cornishware, with a Fairtrade macchiato in a compostable cup in my hand.

I was in the county capital of spelt, surrounded by homespun women in rainbow jumpers with apple-cheeked children. Although we were given a warm welcome among the converted and enlightened, it was so cold I excused myself from leafleting and dove into the market to buy a vest and contemplate a stall selling vegan pasties.

As I was coming back to our HQ by Brioche, I bumped into two teenage girls in pigtails, who were walking around the market carrying a huge U-shaped soft toy, which ended in outstretched hands and splayed fingers. "What is this?" I asked as they wrapped the golden plush around me.

"It's a hug; we are a body-positive collective," they told me as I struggled to breathe. "We spread hugs and tell people to love their bodies as they are."

A man in cords who I wouldn't have sworn had daily acquaintance with the gym paused at the sight of me enfolded into the soft toy with the two girls. "Come and have a group hug," I called to him. "Do you love your body as it is?"

I met just one Leaver in Totnes (even though 54 per cent of the constituency voted Leave). He ran the pet stall. He told me he used to work on the railways, and immigration was unfair. "Why?" I asked.

"Immigrants work for less, they put locals out of work, and they send money back to their own countries rather than spend it here," he said.

"Yes, but they still pay more in taxes overall than they take in state support," I said, "so they are net contributors."

"I know," said the Totnes Leaver.

This made me think. To what extent were low incomes—whether they were lowered or not by the rich and ready supply of willing workers from the EU—the trigger for Brits to think, "Fuck it, I'm scraping by, what's to lose," and want out? The average salary in the United States was around $48,000 (£37,000) in 2018. The average income in the U.K. in 2019 is around £28,000. With the pound sinking to parity against the dollar and the euro, the British worker takes home far less than the American wage earner does. No wonder, when faced with the choice of doing nothing or sticking up two fingers to the man, 52 per cent chose the latter course. Brexit was voted for by those who lost nothing (the hedge funders, the disaster capitalists, you name it) and those who had nothing to lose, as in the Kris Kristofferson song "Me and Bobby McGee." Freedom's just another word for nothing left to lose . . .

As I was leaving the pet stall, a man swooshed past in a turquoise velvet swagger coat, his wild black Medusa-like hair bound in a yellow brocade turban. Your average Totnessian, in other words. I thought he would be a walkover. I tried to hand him a leaflet and canvass him for his vote, but he was having none of it.

"I don't believe in politics," he said, swaggering past towards Neal's Yard Remedies. "I believe in earth, wind, and fire."

Then a man in full pirate costume with sideburns and a bushy black goatee came up to the stall. He explained he didn't vote either.

"Why?" I asked.

"Because I am led by music and love," he answered. That seemed not a good enough answer.

"You've got stuff in your beard," I pointed out cruelly. "What's your name?"

"Elijah," he said, his fingers combing through the excrescence for foreign bodies.

"And what do your parents call you?" I said. I had a feeling.

"Dylan," he admitted.

After leafleting in the cold, Sarah Wollaston insisted on taking us all to a pizza lunch by the Dart. Jo's brother Tim McCarron carried on filming.

"When you are a candidate, you pay for everything, and you

don't reclaim expenses," she confirmed as the various bubbling pizzas were brought to us on wooden boards. "But you should count yourselves lucky. It costs about £40,000 to become an MP. If you make it, you work far harder than you did in your old job, then everyone is vile to you. What people who criticise and troll you don't know is, you have paid through the nose to work for them, and all you get is a cascade of shit that invades every part of your life."

Thick of It Moment 6: One of my very first acts as a prospective candidate was to post a picture of my cream tea (I wanted to show off I had baked the scones myself). This caused a small war on social media, as the country divides not just on the pronunciation of the word *scone* but also as to what comes first, the cream or the jam (it's cream first in Devon and Somerset, for example, but NOT in Cornwall). "Well done, you've lost the Cornish vote," someone replied and tweeted me a picture of a tube of Anusol with the caption "The only cream that should go on the bottom."

· · ·

AFTER TOTNES WE BUZZED OVER TO PLYMOUTH, OR PLYM, as locals call it. We were going to set up the camping table at the Barbican. I drove round and round, lost as usual. The Barbican turned out to be a dockside area patrolled by bored French school trips and gaggles of white-haired Brexiteers in rustling outerwear who told me they "wanted their country back" and didn't want to be run by "faceless Brussels bureaucrats."

It was hard yards. We handed out leaflets to pensioners, but one foursome spotted Sarah Wollaston and formed up to us, bristling. "Oi! Are you that splinter group who left your parties and won't stand in by-elections?" they asked accusingly, as if Sarah were a wanted terrorist.

We nodded.

"Well. You can have your leaflets right back then!" they said, and strewed the pamphlets over the cobbled lanes.

Back home on Exmoor I warmed up the offending scones in one of my two AGAs as Emily Maitlis of *Newsnight* was coming to tea with Alice Thomson of *The Times*. It was Sunday. It felt like the right thing to do.

A shiny Land Rover zoomed into the yard, splattered with mud and cow pat. *The Times*'s crack interviewer Alice Thomson was at the wheel, looking about fourteen in a pastel-blue cashmere jersey and jeans and wellies, and far too young to be in charge of a motor vehicle.

Emily, the Queen of the Night, was in go-faster black leggings, a black crop top, and yellow neon singlet, looking very whizzy. Turquoise wellies and matching wellie socks. I took them to my father's longhouse, I showed them the barns and the duck pond, and then we came back and ate the scones in the garden.

We sat on the grass gossiping about Gavin Williamson, who had just been sacked, and also the meaning of the local elections, which had just happened. Change UK hadn't stood, but it had been a modest triumph for the Lib Dems. Indeed, the big question was, would the Lib Dems—who'd had their best night for a decade—rise phoenixlike from the ashes and in doing so bury Change UK in the Euros, on the grounds that everyone would vote for the tried-and-trusted Remain party with a ground game, not the insurgents without one?

I gave Alice a scone thickly spread with cream and jam.

Emily Maitlis then gave her order, which I carried out to the letter: "lots of cream, first, then not so much jam."

The country may still be divided over Brexit, the issue that neither another referendum nor another general election will ever lay to rest, and poison politics for generations to come, but as we sank our jaws into the scones in satisfied silence, it was clear we had, at least, dealt with the most controversial issue in the South West. It's cream first—and please don't send me angry letters with pictures of haemorrhoid preparations.

The sun went down over the hill, and the garden turned chill.

The two power blondes gave me sympathetic looks (it was clear they thought the results had buried Change UK's chances), thanked me for the scones, told me I was "very brave" (everyone said that; it means they think you are mad), and disappeared down the drive in the gleaming Land Rover Defender, with a kingfisher flash of Emily Maitlis's wellies.

10

The Bubble

DAYS TO ELECTION   17

On May 6, 2019, the town criers and Pearly Kings and World's media went into overdrive.

Meghan Markle at last gave birth. The *Mail* laboured even harder over the bank holiday than the Duchess of Sussex and was delivered of a whopping twenty-three-pager of a "baby souvenir" edition to commemorate the newborn princeling. That morning I marked the occasion by doing an early podcast for *Monocle;* then German TV arrived on the doorstep.

It was the usual thing. They swear blind in advance it will take only half an hour tops, and will disturb only from 9:00 a.m. to 9:30 a.m. Inevitably the doorbell buzzes at 8:20 a.m., and seven people walk in carrying enormous tripods, rigs, and lighting umbrellas and start hoofing furniture out the back door before you've had your first morning cup of tea. They are still in your kitchen at noon as the director insists on doing each take from three angles and adding extra noddy shots. You make a vow never to have crews in your house again.

All the interviewers so far in this campaign said the same,

as if they had conferred in advance. My party had bodged its branding. Everyone was confused: Was it called TIG or Change UK; how do we differ from the Lib Dems? I wearily chanted my stock responses. The party was a start-up, and we were a single-issue party going into this election. Politics seemed to consist of saying the same, not very interesting or convincing things, over and over again.

I glanced at my phone after the German crew had finally gone and put the furniture back and found a message on WhatsApp from the social media team. It appeared they had changed the name of the party . . . again. I actually screamed out loud.

"To further reflect our commitment to our new name Change UK our social handles have been changed from @indgroup," the WhatsApp said. And listed them:

Facebook @ForChangeNow

Twitter @ForChange_Now—that is, not even the same as the Facebook handle, with a dreaded underscore.

I put my head on the desk for a long time. It was the underscore that did it. Then I sent out a message to the whole Change UK group: all the press officers, the social media team (which was being led by the twenty-five-year-old Freddie Chambers, "Rustle" Chambers's son), all the prospective candidates, and all the eleven MPs. "This is an air war and you are sending us into battle with our handles broken for the second time," I wrote. I begged them to keep to the old handles.

What I didn't know then was that the old Tigger handles during the transition to @ForChange_Now had been nabbed by Brexiteer guerrilla accounts who were, even as we were all processing the latest catastrofuck, tweeting out messages like "Remoaners lost, get over it" and "Brexit means Brexit" from our own blue-tick verified account.

You couldn't make it up.

Someone called Roaring Nurse moaned, "Are you kidding me? The old @ has been taken by a Brexiteer?" Someone called Arun added, "All my old tweets link to a Brexit-supporting page."

I called Freddie Chambers, who was dealing with all this on his own for a pittance. "Freddie, this is an air war and we've just lost it," I moaned.

Freddie then sent me a long WhatsApp explaining what had happened, but it was all too clear. Some hostile actor on Twitter had seized the old handle (which had 225,000 followers, twice as many as the Brexit Party) within seconds of the switchover. "Five seconds," Freddie said. "It only took five seconds."

The candidates' WhatsApp group went into meltdown. Most people were beside themselves; others claimed it was all part of the process. "Remain outward-focused, folks! Let's change the United Kingdom—Change UK."

On Twitter, the balls-up started trending.

Whenever the party committed an unforced error—for example, losing its blue-tick verified account with 225,000 followers to a Brexit cell—you could depend on it: one of the battle-hardened eleven MPs would say soothingly, "This is Westminster bubble stuff."

This time it got so bad that Chuka had to come onstream. Our leader in all but name joined the WhatsApp thread, which had gone into meltdown. "I think this is Westminster bubble stuff," he said as I sat in a corner and rocked myself. "What the public care about is that we are anti-Brexit, pro–People's Vote, and pro-Remain."

No, Chuka. I've just been in Plymouth, and they don't care about that. What the public (the white male over-sixties in the South West anyway) care about is that "the people" voted

Out in 2016 and that MPs have failed to deliver on this instruction.

I was so cross I texted Anna Soubry. She texted back to say she was in the chamber. She had had a quick look at her phone and seen the gleeful report on the Guido Fawkes blog that we had changed our name again and been hacked and lost our blue tick and we were a hopeless shower called Change FUKWIT and so on.

"Ach, Guido, they talk of nothing else in Broxtowe," she texted. "It's all about firming up Change UK. It's really not a problem IMHO. It's really important we don't get deflected and distracted by our opponents. We are Change UK for a People's Vote and Remain. Simples."

I had risked what was left of my professional reputation on a party that couldn't even decide what it was called and what it was for and who its leader should be, but it was too late to turn back now.

Two days later, May 8, I had to go to my first grown-up hustings in the South West and face Ann Widdecombe. I felt all the lust for combat of a blind, one-legged slave facing the emperor's hulking pet gladiator in the blood-soaked sand of the Circus Maximus.

I hadn't seen Ann since the weeks we had spent together in the *Big Brother* house the previous year. Apart from once, when I glimpsed her wheeling a little suitcase, head down, at Paddington station. "Ann!" I screamed. She ignored the cry; she must be used to it. "ANN!" I shouted louder.

She looked up. "Rachel!" she said, and trundled over.

"I owe you a drink," I said (in the *BB* house I had a bet with her about the provenance of a quotation, and we agreed the loser would take the other one to the American Bar of the Savoy for a whiskey). She won the bet, but we'd never had our date. There are some people whom you can't help liking—loving—even though you dislike their politics. Ann Widdecombe is not one of them.

Unlike most politicians, she neither likes people nor wants to be liked. She puts principle above people every time. There is something almost noble in her unpleasantness. She is a Millwall politician, in an age of Millwall politics, which is why she was an ideal candidate for the Brexit Party.

I knew even before I set out on the long road to Cornwall that morning that I had lost the hustings. Miss Widdecombe had beaten me in every category before our first scrap. At the outset of this electoral exercise, I accepted that my main—if not only—USP as a candidate for my fledgling party was recognition. When I walk down the street, I hear people whisper, "Boris's sister." With a superhuman effort I don't yell out, "I have a name of my own, you know."

After all, they could be a voter.

Still, you can't underestimate recognition as a plus if you want to stand for election. After all, if you stopped someone in the street, they wouldn't recognise most of the cabinet. One poll in 2015 asked respondents who members of the cabinet were and nobody—not one person—when shown pictures recognised Greg Clark, the minister for communities and local government. I can just imagine it. "Nope. Not me guv. Not a clue. Hancock someone?"

I am a pleaser—I want to say what people want to hear. Classic middle child. But people want conviction politicians. Like Ann Widdecombe. Who tell them they are being told what to do by faceless bureaucrats sitting in large offices in Brussels. That Parliament has stolen their democracy. That the will of the people must be delivered. All messages that cut through.

Plus, Ann had done *Strictly*. Ann does panto. Ann had done *Celebrity Fit Club*. Ergo Ann was next-level box office, almost a national treasure. If her party stayed on 30 per cent in the polls, it was a slam dunk for Ann, and the Brexit Party would clean up.

Quick note on electoral reform.

There is a convention in this country that first past the post (FPTP) will throttle at birth the feeble attempts at independent life from any newborn political party in a general election (GE). This convention was firmly established in 1983, when, as you may remember, the SDP–Liberal Alliance won 25.4 per cent of the vote but only twenty-three seats, and more recently in the 2015 GE, when UKIP snagged 12.6 per cent or around four million votes—a triumph that translated into only one seat for Nigel Farage.

The two-party lock on the political system is entrenched and mirrored in the media and across Westminster. Since the last war, 90 per cent of the U.K. press were badged either Labour or Tory. I can still remember how everyone sniggered when *The Guardian* under Alan Rusbridger, then editor, endorsed the Lib Dems in 2010 (as did the *Indy*). The Lib Dems! It was regarded as so wringingly wet of him that people almost wept with laughter.

Ditto the broadcast media. It is writ that the regulator Ofcom "expects" broadcasters will provide "appropriate" coverage of the tiddlers, the Lib Dems, Greens, Plaid Cymru, and so on, but as the system determines most of the seats are held by the two main parties, this is reflected in their coverage, which divides between Labour and Tory, although since 2016, the broadcasters have also had to balance Leavers with Remainers to reflect the new split in politics.

In Parliament too, small parties suffer as the official opposition is given precedence over third parties when it comes to Commons business. When Change UK's MPs ditched their birth parties, individual politicians' long-held positions on cross-party select committees were threatened. Labour, for example, tried to eject Mike Gapes and Ian Austin from the Foreign Affairs Committee and Chris Leslie from International Trade. Theresa May herself had to step in to protect Sarah Wollaston from being bumped from her important roles as chair of both the Health and Social Care and the Liaison Committees.

All this is to stress that if you're not red and you're not blue, the struggle is real, people.

As I prepped for Falmouth, I knew it was not enough to be a D-lister with a midsized media presence—fifty-eight thousand followers on Twitter, thirteen thousand on Instagram—and recognisable hair. I was heading to Cornwall—56.5 per cent Leave—where the main issue was fishing, and for that reason alone there might be trouble ahead.

Back in June 2016, you see, as the referendum campaign was at its fervid peak, I had joined Bob Geldof on a white pleasure cruiser called *Sarpedon* one Wednesday morning on the Thames. On board there was a ragtag-and-bobtail bunch of fellow noisy Remainers. We sat around eating Kit Kats for a bit, then set off, waving black-and-white banners and flags saying IN on them, while the song "The 'In' Crowd" blared on a loop through loudspeakers.

We were doing this because, at the very same time, Admiral of the Leave Fleet Nigel Farage was leading his own armada of fishing vessels from Ramsgate in Kent up the Thames to moor outside the Houses of Parliament during the final PMQs before the referendum, and we wanted to make a point and intercept him. It would be high profile—two tribes going to war on the river outside Parliament—but beyond that, there's nothing so much fun as messing about in boats. Needless to say, it all went wrong.

The two rival armadas clashed first by Tower Bridge, with Bob Geldof shouting into a megaphone, "You're no FOKKING fisherman's friend! Britain makes more FOKKING money out of fishing than any other in Europe! Britain has the second-largest quota after Denmark! You are on the fishing committee of the European Parliament, and you attended ONE out of forty-three meetings! You're a FOKKING FRAUD, Nigel!"

Police speedboats with frogmen in black wet suits zoomed around and shouted at us, but everyone's blood was up. The great naval battle of the Thames 2016 had been joined.

As it happened, the billionaire media baron Rupert Murdoch was hosting a lunch in the boardroom on the twelfth floor of his News Building overlooking the Thames that day, and one of the guests was the co-leader of the Leave campaign, who arrived the exact moment our two armadas were clashing below by London Bridge.

When he arrived, Boris told me, Rupert and his henchmen were gathered at the plate-glass window, looking down as a police launch was hosing down the fishing smacks and our vessel like a trainer trying to separate a pack of fighting dogs. Fishing boats were chugging alongside, and film crews were rushing to the picturesque scene, which was being livestreamed by a helicopter on Sky and BBC News.

A fishing vessel fluttering the flag of St. George and one saying "The Only Way Is Brexit" came alongside. Some angry Leavers jumped aboard the *Sarpedon* as me and Bob Geldof were dancing a little jig on deck.

"G'day, Boris," Murdoch said. "Have you seen?" He pointed to the *Sarpedon*. "Your little sister appears to be making a nuisance of herself on the river."

We repelled the invaders and came closer to the Houses of Parliament—every bridge was hung with the drooping banners of rival factions, people shouting encouragement and abuse—where a large crowd had gathered on the Commons and Lords terraces.

Bob Geldof resumed his loud harangue, which he concluded by flipping the bird at Farage and Kate Hoey, who were on some sort of barge within yards of our vessel. Unfortunately, it looked as if the millionaire pop star activist were insulting the humble fisherfolk, not Farage.

"We used to protest against the establishment, now the establishment protests against us," the People's Nigel told the BBC later, piously, in a clip that went viral.

It was of course great fun, but thanks to Bob's V sign the stunt backfired and it looked as if we were protesting against the hardworking fisherfolk, not the Lords of Leave.

The day I was due in Falmouth, a man tweeted, "I never knew Rachel Johnson took part in Bob Geldof's Flotilla of the Wankers. That'll go down well with Fishing communities in the South West!" It had more than a thousand retweets, so rolled the pitch for my Cornish debut nicely.

· · ·

THE *TODAY* PROGRAMME'S POLITICAL REPORTER ROSS Hawkins had been calling me to ask whether he could stalk me around the West Country stump. I am as everyone knows a shy, modest person who guards my privacy fiercely and abhors personal publicity, so I'd said, "Weeeeell. I'm in Falmouth Wednesday doing a hustings with the Brexit Party's Ann Widdecombe and the Tories and the Labour councillor and . . ." I trailed off. I couldn't remember, nor did Ross care.

There were so many candidates, so little time. I was living on GWR trains.

"I'll see you in Falmouth, then," Hawkins suggested. "Shall we say 3:00 p.m. at Rick Stein's?"

We were both coming from London. I was up early to do media. I'd said yes to BBC 5 Live at the Millbank studio with the presenter Emma Barnett. I didn't know the other guest was Ann Widdecombe, who was "down the line" in a remote studio and with whom I was husting later (I presume "husting" is a verb as well as a noun).

I lugged my overnight bag for the Cornwall trip into the studio with me. Emma Barnett, in a leopard-skin wrap dress and trainers, specs, and tumbling blond locks, asked all the same questions as everyone else. Why do you keep changing your name? Why on earth have you called yourself "Change" when your only policy is to keep everything the same? Why haven't you joined up with the other Remain parties so you don't split the vote?

Basically why are you lot such a shower?

She was only doing her job, but I felt that ever since I'd joined the party, I'd been on the back foot. I just wanted to make jokes to lighten the mood, like "Yes, we should have called ourselves Status Quo" and so on, but I didn't. Jokes never work.

"Look. Think of the launch of Change UK like this," I told the 5 Live audience. "Meghan wanted to have a lovely home birth at Frogmore Cottage, but nature had other plans, and she was medevacked to the Portland. Things don't always go smoothly." After that, every time I tried to open my mouth, Ann went, "Let me finish!" or "I did Rachel the COURTESY"—rolling her r's in that annoying pronounced way—"of listening to her speak, now it's MY TURN," for what seemed like ages.

As she pointed out, her party was smashing it in the polls and mine was trailing. I had a comeback to this up my sleeve, like a bit of shrivelled Kleenex. "Look at the semifinal of the Champions League last night," I said, knowing full well that Ann would not have watched it, but the 5 Live audience would. "Liverpool manager Jürgen Klopp didn't have key strikers Mo Salah or Roberto Firmino, his team was trailing Barca 3–0 on aggregate. Yet he was 1–0 up at halftime, and Liverpool won the match against all odds 4–0," I concluded, "so if they can do it, we can do it."

Ann clearly had no idea what I was talking about, as this shut her up for the first time in the entire discussion.

"Well done getting the two main news stories of the week— the Champions League semis and the royal baby—into the ten-minute chat," Emma Barnett purred. "Typical journalist."

I left Millbank at a run to do Chopper's—that is, *The Telegraph*'s Christopher Hope's—Brexit podcast. This is always recorded in the cellar of the Red Lion pub at Derby Gate.

I sat over hot café au lait and talked a blue streak. I called the Brexit Party the "home of the Whopper," à la Burger King, because Farage trades in lies, and then I ran to Westminster tube to get the underground to Victoria. As I was boarding the Gatwick Express at Victoria, I had a text from Flybe saying my flight from LHR to Newquay had been delayed to 1:28 p.m. I stared at my screen. A warning bell tinkled somewhere in a distant chamber of my cerebellum.

LHR . . . LHR . . . that meant HEATHROW, not Gatwick.

The train doors were closing. I inserted myself in the jaws and squeezed out of the Gatwick Express just in time.

I shall spare you most of the traditional 'mare that was my long trip to Cornwall. I pelted out of Victoria station in a monsoon. Have you ever tried to get a cab or Uber at Victoria station in a monsoon? You cannot.

I went back down into the bowels of the tube in despair. Tube staff helpfully advised that the best way to Heathrow would be Victoria line to Oxford Circus, change to Bakerloo line to Paddington, then Heathrow Express. It was so crowded people were crushed into the stairwell.

There were no trains announced on the board.

I waited.

It was 11:15 a.m. My flight had been delayed, but the text said that check-in still closed at noon.

Then the announcement came that the next train would be in twenty-five minutes. I rushed out of the station again, and this time a black cab took pity as my third Uber had sailed past me, soaking me in brown puddle and pretending he hadn't seen me. In the cab, I shook myself like a dog and saw a text from the *Today* programme's reporter Ross Hawkins. "I'm in Falmouth early. Just shout if you're in town and we can do the i/v sooner, Ross."

I was still in London.

"Ross chaos here and might miss plane," I texted back. I left out the fact that I had been about to go to the wrong airport.

"But you're definitely coming even if late? Have built piece about you," Hawkins replied. The sainted cabbie got me to Terminal Two in thirty minutes. I could have kissed him.

I sailed magically fast through security and passport control, and when I got to the lounge, I checked the departure board. An old reflex. Obviously, I must have missed the plane and would have to let down the *Today* programme. But by my flight it said, "Go to Gate."

The unbearable hope returned.

At the gate, a surfer dude was sprawled on the ground, charging his laptop. The rest of the passengers seemed almost somnolent. The plane hadn't yet boarded. I was so relieved that I did what I always do: I went to get a celebratory coffee from Pret, from where I called Ivo. I gave him the brief edited lowlights of the past hour. "Stop," he begged, "just the fact that you got on the Gatwick Express is making my blood pressure spike!"

I finished my sorry tale. "Okay, you made it to Heathrow," he said in an odd voice. "What gate are you at?"

I checked, suddenly in a panic that I had missed the flight after all that to get a flat white.

"1A," I told him. "Why?"

"Well, I'm at Gate 2A," he said, reminding me he had told me several times he was going to Edinburgh that day. I had no memory of any such conversation. "Look, I'm waving! Over here. We could have shared a taxi."

11

Falmouth

DAYS TO ELECTION 15

When I got to Newquay, I was a dehydrated husk (I am too green—and mean—to buy bottled water for £3). I had delayed my rendezvous with the *Today* programme reporter until 4:00 p.m. and was waiting in Rick Stein's. After about thirty minutes, two burly men with purposeful expressions and military miens entered the quayside "eatery."

"Table for five at five," one said.

Then Ann Noreen Widdecombe walked in wearing a faux Chanel white bouclé jacket and a splashy blue Brexit Party rosette, flanked by her bodyguards. Even though we had already clashed our antlers on the airwaves that day, she appeared not to see me standing by the bar, the only other person in the restaurant. She was going everywhere with a car and a driver and security detail, while I was paying all my own expenses—I had just splashed 50 quid on a black cab to Heathrow—and didn't have so much as a Change UK *badge*.

"Hello, Ann," I said.

I have seen Ann in her nightie; I know her snore the way a mother ewe knows her baby lamb by its bleat. I have brought her tea and biscuits in bed. Yet she did not even give me a courtesy nod. I decided she hadn't heard me—maybe we are all going a little deaf—and approached her table, where she sat sandwiched between her heavies. "Why the security, Ann?" I asked, but she just shook her head.

When she'd had a piece of bread, Ann softened enough to tell me that a fellow Brexit Party candidate, the salmon magnate Lance Forman, had had a swastika daubed on the side of his shed, as if that explained why the Brexit Party was taking no chances with the health and safety of the star of *Celebrity Fit Club* and *Strictly*.

Ross Hawkins appeared just as Ann was tucking into her "mains" of sea bream fillets. I had made a mental plan to make Ross interview me in the Quayside Inn next door and perhaps have my own early fish supper there on the BBC (a TripAdvisor review said, "Laid-back pub serving hearty fare amid wood floors," which sounded perfect). Ross, however, insisted we do a walkabout in town. He refused even to stop for a pale Cornish ale in the pub as a stiffener for the ordeal of the televised hustings in a university theatre that lay ahead. He route-marched me through Falmouth, past chandlers and shops selling matelot jerseys I was longing to rootle in, seagulls crying and wheeling above our heads.

After about ten minutes we paused for breath on a pier. I felt faint and panted as we gazed over the fishing-boat-bobbing harbour, grateful for the pit stop. There had been a rapid-fire back-and-forth as we walked through the narrow streets. I had explained my position on centrism, the failure of liberalism, and how important it was that the Remain resistance didn't crumble.

"So what is it about the Lib Dems that made you drop them?"

Ross asked. "Name a policy you disagree with." He thrust the mic in my face.

When I saw the red light blinking on his device, it was as if it switched off my brain.

One, I couldn't name a single Lib Dem policy apart from tuition fees.

Two, Change UK hadn't published its own policy document yet.

The seconds ticked by.

"Long pause," Ross teased after about seven or eight seconds.

"I'm just enjoying the view, Ross," I managed to say.

After the interview, I got a cab to the Penryn Campus. During the ride I went through my phone. The South West WhatsApp group was pumped; the actual ballot paper had come through. Thanks to Farage calling his party not "Brexit Party" but "The Brexit Party," Change UK was first on the ballot paper, as parties are listed alphabetically. Therefore, on four million ballot papers across vast swaths of the country, my name was FIRST. Someone wrote, "That must be worth at least 10 per cent of the vote," in a hopeful way.

"Rachel Sabiha Johnson Change UK The Independent Party," it says.

Underneath me, the five other members of the slate are listed in the correct order, then the Conservative and Unionist Party, then some folk called the English Democrats, the Green Party, the Labour Party, the Liberal Democrats, The Brexit Party, UKIP, and three Independents. Apart from the indies, each party had fielded six candidates, and the next time we would all be gathered together in one place would be the declaration in Poole on May 26.

I sent the screenshot of the ballot paper to my father. I couldn't think of anyone else who would be remotely interested.

"Top of the ballot paper, bottom of the polls," I wrote alongside the picture.

Penryn Campus, which turned out confusingly to be part of the University of Exeter, was lush. Views over the Fal estuary. Landscaped grounds. Clean modern canteens, and home, I learned, to the £30 million Environment and Sustainability Institute as well as a Renewable Energy Facility (acronym "REEF"). This was hopeful. In common with key bits of the westernmost county of the U.K. and my putative constituency, much of this gleaming educational real estate had been funded by the EU. Maybe the audience would, gosh, I don't know, look around them and think that maybe, maybe, they might be onto a good thing?

I did back-to-back interviews, blogs, podcasts, for various student and local outlets in different bits of the uni, then went into the theatre. I took my seat alongside the other five candidates, including Widdy. Showtime.

I scanned the audience. A sea of white hair. Bad news. In my experience, many people over sixty-eight or so are nostalgic for the Britain of pre-1973—that is, pre our entry into the EEC. They want spinsters on bicycles, warm beer, nobody with a "funny tinge" speaking "foreign" languages on trains, and they blame everything that's wrong with the country on Brussels or "brown people flooding the NHS," as someone told me in Plymouth. Even my own darling mother (DOB 1942) voted Leave. I rest my case.

Some of the audience were in navy fishermen's smocks. This was very concerning. I could only pray none of them knew—or recalled—my "Flotilla of the Wankers" Bob Geldof escapade.

The Labour woman on the panel was very good and pointed out that 80 per cent of the Cornish catch goes to the EU, particularly France. What would happen when they didn't have frictionless trade into the main market for their biggest perishable export?

I tried saying that in all we export £274 billion worth of goods and services to the EU, worth around 15 per cent of the economy, and our next nearest trading partner was the United States, to which we sent £112 billion—my point being we did most of our trade with the bloc on the doorstep, ergo it would be self-defeating to throw up barriers—but that didn't cut through. Nobody appeared to give a stuff. They all hated the Common Fisheries Policy. "We want our waters back," they cried at intervals whenever I opened my mouth.

Democracy and sovereignty don't butter any parsnips, I tried saying, but consider this: the EU had stumped up a billion pounds for Cornwall to fund the Eden Project, superfast broadband, the airport I'd flown to, Cornwall Airport Newquay, the dualling of the A30, and even the very swanky theatre and campus the event was being held in; then Widdy cut in.

"Yes, the EU is spending a BILLION pounds of OURRRRR money!" shrilled Ann Widdecombe, to a roar of applause. Thus my point that Cornwall voting Leave was a classic example of turkeys voting for Christmas AND Thanksgiving was drowned out by Ann Widdecombe's fake news that all EU money was ours alone.

At the end, a couple of people came up to tell me some very important things: they had been at Sherborne with my father, or one of my brothers had given their grandson work experience and both were capital chaps. It is an iron rule of my life that at least three people in any room have met at least one Johnson male and have to pass on as much detailed information to me about their interaction with said Johnson on a need-to-know basis.

I fled. A kind student drove me to Truro station in her little car, CDs littering the footwell. I was an hour early for the sleeper train, so headed to the pub. The Railway Tavern was a grungy dive with sticky carpets and a sign saying, "No Children Stood or Sat the Bar." (Almost as bad as Prince Harry saying "Myself and Meghan are thrilled" a couple of days earlier at the birth of Archie Harrison Mountbatten-Windsor.)

I had a half of bitter and a greasy homemade sausage roll with bacon and cheese and got chatting to the men playing pool. "Nah, May's deal ain't no good," one said, as he chalked his tip and aimed the cue at the pink. Another iron rule: there is no other conversation but Brexit from Land's End to John o' Groat's.

"Too Leave for Remainers, too Remain for Leavers. Not the proper job at all."

I got on the Cornish Riviera from Truro at 10:29 p.m. in a state of toddler excitement. I romped around my couchette, got into my pj's, then put in my earplugs and affixed my eye mask, and rocked my way gently east, arriving at Paddington at 6:50 a.m. When I woke, we had come to a final station stop and were berthed in Platform One, and most people had left the train.

I put on the radio on my iPhone for the *Today* programme as I got up and, as luck would have it, Ross Hawkins's package from Falmouth was on. The first thing I heard back in London was my "sound of silence" clip on the *Today* programme.

My iPhone buzzed with people saying, "I heard your magisterial interview on *Today*" with crying-laughing-face emoji. My Pinterish pause was much mocked on various political blogs. *The Spectator* put up a story straightaway:

It seems inevitable that the European elections this month will be seen as a litmus test of the British public's attitude to Brexit, especially when it comes to a second referendum. And, if Nigel Farage's Brexit Party triumphs over the Remain coalition, the case for a People's Vote will be weaker than ever.

So as you can imagine, the Lib Dems and Greens (as two parties backing a second referendum) are deeply unhappy that a third, Change UK, has joined the fray and will further split the Remain vote on 23 May.

They may be even unhappier though when they realise that Change UK candidates aren't even sure why they're not Lib Dems. The Change UK MEP candidate for south-west England, Rachel Johnson, was interviewed by Radio 4 this morning, and suggested that her new party was a "fresh alternative to the Lib Dems."

Yet when asked by the BBC's Ross Hawkins if she could name a single Lib Dem policy she disagreed with, the Johnson sibling was lost for words. A remarkable ten-second silence followed, before Johnson eventually had to concede that she was simply "enjoying the view."

The Spectator helpfully provided a "listen here" link so that readers could enjoy my emission for themselves. It was repeated on the *World at One* and various other media outlets. The *Express* pounced as it always did.

"Rachel Johnson, the sister of Boris Johnson, is standing as a candidate for Change UK in the upcoming European elections at the end of May. But the Remain supporter, who was a member of the Liberal Democrats because of Brexit, was left SILENCED after a BRUTAL question by a BBC political correspondent."

Whatever happened on May 26, I could at least lay claim to the shortest career—but longest broadcast pause—in recent British political history.

P.S. The Pause even had an afterlife.

Nick Robinson put it into his *Political Thinking* podcast, and when I went into Broadcasting House that Sunday, a studio manager told me he'd had to shorten it by several seconds. This was because there was a risk that if they played it in full, the "emergency tape" would kick in, which is what happens if the station falls off air or there's a nuclear strike. I refuse to be embarrassed by it. In a campaign desperately needing wins, it felt like an achievement.

12

Millbank

DAYS TO ELECTION 14

Two Thursdays before polling day, there were three things in the diary: a dinner at the Design Museum for the launch of the Kubrick exhibition and an after-dinner shakedown at a donors' dinner; then I was booked to appear on *This Week* with Andrew Neil, the late late politics show that goes out on BBC One after *Question Time*—that is, in the middle of the night, just around the time that producers for the *Today* programme are getting up.

I had to locate an outfit, therefore, that would "transition" from Design Museum via a Soho boardroom to the BBC studio. I chose navy pin-striped cigarette pants from H&M and a bright blue jersey from Zara (the entire outfit less than £30), which I thought was a result until I arrived at the Design Museum to find A-list celebs twirling on a special *Clockwork Orange*–style tunnel for the paparazzi as they made their entries.

Ah. Nobody had warned me the dress code for the Kubrick dinner was "glamorous." The photographers' long lenses drooped at my entrance, as they would, as all the other women were in on-trend shimmering midi dresses from Net-a-Porter with designer platform trainers.

The party was upstairs, but I wanted to see the show. As I wandered past galleries of droogs and collected shelves of the director's notebooks, there were only two other guests not getting stuck into the champagne. They were Tony Hall, the chairman of the BBC, and his wife, Cynthia—or as I still call her, "Mrs. Hall," as she used to be my A-level English teacher. We stood talking about gender imbalance at the BBC while gazing at the "erotic furniture" from the Korova Milk Bar in *A Clockwork Orange*.

At dinner, I sat next to a kindly lawyer called Hugh Devlin who had trendy adman glasses. He was handed a special plate with his "mains" of pink roast beef with so much fuss and fanfare that I had to ask what was different about his. "I always tell caterers *in advance* that I cannot abide the taste of celery," he said.

"But there isn't any celery," I said, looking at my plate.

"Ah, yes, I found out that the gravy is made with a stock that contained celery. I can taste celery in gravy," he said, shuddering. "Fennel, however, I can tolerate."

I told him that when I am asked if I have any "dietaries," I always reply, "Yes. Food."

Jeremy Irons, the actor, was lugubrious and thin-lipped. "I'm trying to get some summer in Ireland this year," he drawled in his chocolaty voice.

"Isn't Irish summer an oxymoron?" I asked, wondering whether to add it to my list of pet oxymorons: jobs-first Brexit, American cheese, Hershey's chocolate, managed no deal, fun run, compassionate conservatism, and so on.

I ordered an Uber, as I reckoned I had to be in Soho at 9:30 p.m. This was important.

We needed at least £3,000 to make it to polling day to keep the slate crisscrossing the South West on expensive GWR trains for hustings, cheese tastings, Gloucester 4 Remain events, and farmers' markets in Stroud. . . . This dinner was my last chance to perform open-wallet surgery and keep the show on the road before the election.

I got out of the taxi at a groovy ad agency, Johnny Hornby's The&Partnership, in an after-hours Soho, with revellers staggering from bar to bar. There were no signs of life apart from a man sitting behind a swish desk. The doors were locked. I stood at the large glass doors and waved. He shook his head.

I waved again. He got up heavily from behind his desk.

"Who are you and what do you want?" he said as I came in. It was a bad start, but this didn't register. I was in too much of a hurry.

"Where's the dinner?" I asked as I clattered towards the lift on the heels I had put on in the Prius with rapid purpose.

In my own mind I was seconds away from making a grand entrance into some cool upstairs boardroom. There, Heidi, Chuka, Leslie, Soubs, and sundry passionate, deep-pocketed Europhiles would be waiting for me to blow them all away with my pitch and shake them down for six-figure donations, and then I would sail off to Millbank to be sandpapered by Mr. A. F. Neil as they gazed at my departing back in wonder and praise.

"What dinner?" the night watchman replied. The gentleman had gone back to the football on his iPad under the desk. My heart sank.

I called Johnny Hornby from a trendy sofa in reception. He didn't pick up. I called Elle, the press person. She didn't pick up.

I sat for an hour, then ordered another Uber and left for Millbank. As I cruised through the wet London night, the smooth tarmac gleaming like liquorice down the Strand, I realised I'd left a dinner with Benedict Cumberbatch . . . Nigella Lawson . . . Harry Enfield . . . Elizabeth McGovern! before pudding! to sit in a lobby with a night watchman who, when I asked him if I could watch the Chelsea match with him on his iPad under the desk while I waited for time to pass, said no.

It was not good prep for *This Week* with Andrew Neil, the one telly show that no member of the cabinet will go on—and with reason. One, it goes out live at almost midnight and you are inevitably refreshed by the time you are "sat" in front of the grand inquisitor. Two, nobody really gets out alive. Andrew Neil is a lean, mean, grilling machine—the George Foreman of interviewers.

God knows why I agreed to it. Actually I do know. This is why.

I do *Question Time* and other shows of that ilk so that other women see me being not very good, under-rehearsed, and so on, and think, "Well, Rachel Johnson was terrible, and anyway what's with her hair?" and realise that maybe you don't have to be perfect every time you open your mouth or appear in public. You can be average and look crap and that's okay too.

If you talk to the producers of shows like *Question Time, Any Questions,* and *Have I Got News for You,* they will tell you, to a man, that they ask women to go on these shows all the time. It's women who always knock them back and refuse. (I did *HIGNFY* again in October 2019, and the nicest reaction I got was the person who tweeted, "Rachel Johnson was funny but not as funny as when she tweeted that Cameron was an egg-faced cunt.")

I sat in the greenroom—that is, a poky gully with no wine or crisps. Andrew Neil breezed by. Liz Kendall, MP, one of the regulars, sat at a computer in the newsroom. My eyelids were drooping. The studio manager came to fetch me and I went on set, where Liz was sitting squished up against Michael Portillo, looking mooby in a pink shirt.

Andrew Neil welcomed me, then let me have it.

"Two hours ago, Rachel, you were a Lib Dem!" he berated me.

Then he gave me both barrels as Liz and Portillo shifted uncomfortably and stared around the set, not catching my eye.

"You're an amateur outfit whose only success to date is dividing the Remain vote and fighting among yourselves. . . . It's a vanity project for MPs. You're useless. You're undemocratic. Your only policy is to overturn the referendum result and the Lib Dems have been working on that for three years and you jumped-up no-hopers . . ."

I smiled in panic and hoped sweat wasn't showing under my jersey, which was the tight acrylic blue jersey with little gold buttons on the cuffs from Zara that I hoped would distract the viewer because the truth was, everything he said was a fair cop.

In desperation I wheeled out my birth-plan analogy yet again for Andrew "Brillo" Neil (he is thus called because his hair is said to resemble a Brillo pad). "Meghan Markle wanted to have a natural home birth at Frogmore Cottage," I told a boggling Brillo, "but ended up being medevacked to the Portland Hospital! Anyone who has ever given birth," I continued, "which I don't think includes you, Andrew, knows that there is many a slip twixt cup and lip."

Neil pretended to be completely baffled by this and kept turning to the camera and to Portillo as if in mock disbelief.

I was on for only a few minutes around midnight, but it felt as if I'd been several rounds with Tyson Fury. At one point, I opened my mouth to say something, but Neil held up his hand as if stopping traffic and said, "Please, please don't talk about childbirth again."

I reeled out of the studio, didn't even stop for the traditional warm glass of Blue Nun served with crisps that is the extent of the *This Week* after-party. Instead, I carved myself a slice of chewy lemon drizzle cake that the editor of the show had baked himself. I stuffed it in my mouth as I ran down the two blue-carpeted flights of wide stairs and got into my waiting car in the rain. I would be home by 1:45 a.m.

A clip of my comparing the launch of a new party to the birth of Baby Sussex was already attracting ridicule from the *Spectator* blog. I was subjected to the usual pile-on. Was I drunk? Did I speak English? Twitter asked.

"Never been so totally underwhelmed by anyone on the show! Plenty of guests whose opinions differ from mine but @RachelSJohnson was just a complete waste of words in whatever strange order she arranged them! How disappointing," said one happy customer, tagging @bbcthisweek @RachelSJohnson @afneil.

As I sat in the car, I had raging *esprit d'escalier* as ever and realised what I should have said. When told that Change UK was splitting the vote and undermining the Lib Dems, I could have argued, "Why can't you have more than one Remain party? Nobody says Asda and Sainsbury's have to merge. In fact, they've just been told they can't by the Monopolies and Mergers Commission. Think how many Brexit parties there are to choose from. LABOUR. The TORIES. The BREXIT Party. UKIP."

But I didn't, and I fear that nothing I said on *This Week* "landed," as we must say now.

Thick of It Moment 7: Took a sleeping pill, put my iPhone on Do Not Disturb mode, and overslept—missing three calls from the council to say that I'd parked my Volvo illegally and had been towed.

· · ·

ON SATURDAY, I DROVE TO DULWICH FOR A LUNCH. I SHOULD have been in Stroud at a rally, but the Change UK battlebus hadn't turned up yet. Among the guests were the flop-haired political editor of ITV, Robert Peston, a.k.a. Pesto, who was also at the *FT* with us, and his rangy blond girlfriend, Charlotte Edwardes, in high-waisted matelot trousers. Also present were Matt Garrahan of the *FT* and Anna Murphy, the fashion editor of *The Times*, wearing a blue denim jacket with glittery purple appliqué patches, a mauve midi-dress, and Birkenstocks.

"Is what you're wearing . . . fashion?" I asked. I never know.

We gossiped all through lunch, and I couldn't resist chewing the fat with Pesto over a platter piled with pulled pork. I told him that Sarah Wollaston thinks we're not going to get any MEPs. Even Gavin Esler was only on 7 per cent in London. Guido Fawkes, the political blogger, was also counting us out, saying, "If we can't win there, the Chukas can't win anywhere."

"How many Labour Remain votes do you think we can scrape up?" I asked Peston.

After all, there must be millions of Labour Remainers who won't vote Lib Dem. Or Tory. Or Brexit. Or UKIP. I went on: "If there were around four million Remain Labour voters—and five million Labour Leave voters—a big chunk of them surely would tick our box?"

Everyone stopped eating as they waited for the oracle to pronounce.

"Whaat?" Pesto roared, in mid-chew. "None!" he said. "They'll all vote Green! They hate Chuka like poison for being a neo-Blairite! Labour will literally vote for anything but you lot!"

In his considered opinion, most Corbynistas would vote for Farage before they voted for Chuka.

As I left Dulwich to go home, I said to the assembled guests who had mainly aggregated from south of the river, some on foot, "Anyone want a lift back to London?" emphasising "London" in order to burnish my already shining credentials as a metropolitan, elitist snob.

WhatsApp of the Day from the Candidates' Group: "Can anyone come to Basingstoke Station tomorrow Sunday to leaflet at seven a.m.? We will have a BBC camera crew there."

13

Bath

Thursday, May 16, is a gala, red-letter day in the South West slate's calendar. In theory.

Three of the four candidates in the South West—me, Liz Sewell, and Ollie Middleton—had been asked to headline the Bath rally that has been in the diary since day one. I had not yet written a speech, mainly because Elle from head office kept sending me WhatsApps asking to see the "text" of my "speech."

I was supposed to be in Bath at noon, but I still managed to squeeze in a couple of sets of tennis in London with David Cameron, the writer Daisy Waugh, and my brother Jo. We won the first set, as usual; then DC said, "Remember! This one matters as much as the last one!" and "We mustn't be one-set wonders again" as he always does, and then, as we always do, we lost the second set. I think it is because David Cameron's default setting is "lucky general" mode and therefore still suffers—in tennis as in politics—from the assumption of victory.

I had to take my Bath outfit to the tennis club. The morning polls had us on 2 per cent ("As much as that?" Ivo joked as I left), so I felt a bit flat-footed on the court. As we played outside in the sunshine, I couldn't even put away the easy ones. It felt like an omen.

Afterwards, we sat on the terrace, and DC held forth in a loud voice about the political situation without ever owning his part in the horror show. (Since around then, I should note, members have complained about the architect of the omnishambles ruining their leisure time. I have had a formal warning to desist from loose loud talk of Brexit and politics with the former PM on the terrace.)

I told everyone over coffee I was off to Bath to give the first political speech of my life at a Change UK rally.

"And last, I expect," I said.

"Your party looks useless to me, but maybe I've been on Twitter too much," Cameron agreed, as he forked some of my scrambled egg.

"All that hopey-changey stuff worked for me in 2005, but"— he allowed us to witness a brief but not contrite frown—"we are living in different times. The Lib Dems have the momentum after the locals. Change UK or whatever it's called? You shoulda been more Labour Lite. Less Soubry."

"Bad luck, Rake," said Jo as I got up from the table.

"Thank you for your support," I said, and went down to change into my green frock for the rally.

In the queue at Paddington to go through the gates for the 10:30 to Bath Spa, I stood ahead of two men who made my heart sink into my white-and-green Stan Smith trainers. They were John Crace of *The Guardian* and Henry Deedes of the *Mail*. It was like a scene from *Scoop*. But where was Boot of the *Beast*?

"No Quentin Letts?" I asked, scanning the crowd for *The Times*'s sketch writer. (There had been a blog doing the rounds called "The Ditching of Dacre" in July 2018. All suspected the little hatchet of Letts, who hero-worshipped Paul Dacre, his *Daily Mail* editor of many years. The author of it called Geordie Greig a "suck-up" and a "small man with a thin voice" and said of me, "Johnson represents pretty much everything that Dacre hates in journalism." The anonymous author of this charming piece went on to say of his hero Dacre that if I followed Geordie Greig from *The Mail on Sunday* to the *Mail,* "The mere thought of her setting up camp in the pages of his newspaper must make him shake with rage.")

If Letts was here, in Bath, that was it. I would be toast.

"No Letts," said John Crace. "He's doing Farage somewhere up in the North East."

I got into a carriage far from the two sketch writers and reassessed the situation.

I had intended to say a few passionate words about what Europe meant to me. About how I had been a good little European, man and boy, the granddaughter of immigrants, the daughter of a Eurocrat, the product of French, German, Jewish, Russian, and Turkish blood. In terms of serious content, I had an exclusive "I once met a forty-year-old black man in Plymouth" section up my sleeve. I'd recently met an Aussie in his sixties on the Eurostar who had quizzed me about Brexit in bemusement. He ran a haulage company.

"All my drivers tell me it's easier to drive across the whole of the EU than it is from one end of Australia to another," he said, explaining that each Oz state had different regimes and what a bore it all was. "Why are you doing this? Strewth! You have it so good. You guys must be out of yer minds."

Then I had a few nuts and bolts planned on the impact of EU structural funds in the South West . . . how the main market for spring lambs of hill farmers and Cornish fish was the EU . . . some soaring oratory about the four freedoms . . . and I would end with a clarion call to vote Change UK on May 23 and give the rallying cry that *la lucha* must *continua*—as if Change UK descended in a direct line from the antifascists in 1930s Spain.

It seemed okay when I tried it on Ivo in the kitchen at home. But now, sitting on the train, I had my doubts. Fleet Street's finest would be in the audience. I ditched my speech and dug a piece of paper out of my bag and jotted some thoughts down. They wanted red meat, I knew. They wanted colour! They wanted Miss Johnson's Debut Stump Blue-Plate Early Bird Special! Otherwise they had nothing to write, I reckoned. I scribbled away until I felt sick.

The slate met outside Bath Spa station. It was actually my third trip to Bath in the last month or so, even if the first was to spend the day with a group of Norland nannies in a lofty campus overlooking the elegant golden swoosh of Royal Crescent for *The Sunday Times Magazine.*

The second was to leaflet. Make no mistake, leafleting is awful—a universally unpopular activity for all concerned, a form of political chugging. People avoid your gaze. They quicken pace, they pelt towards a *Big Issue* seller, anything not to have to engage. As Sarah Wollaston said as we chased a couple over Bath's famous shop-lined Pulteney Bridge, "People are either actively hostile or extremely interested."

"And both are awful," I said.

It had been in Bath that I met my first out-and-out racist, a peevish pensioner clutching a Sainsbury's carrier bag who said, "What I want is for all the foreign people who I pay my taxes to subsidise and who have taken our jobs to go away again," his pink pate reddening and glistening in the May heat outside M&S. And then he said it.

"I want my country back." I found myself engaging with him and pointed out that immigrants were net contributors to the economy, but as I talked, I noticed he had a pair of brown leather shoes in his carrier bag and wondered what he was going to do with them. Was there a local cobbler? I felt like asking, to change the subject.

As the campaign has worn on, the truth seemed to be that if you scratched the surface/lifted the stone, quite a lot of people secretly think like this, but only a very few, like the Bald Man of Bath, will say it out loud. I considered whether it was people like him who'd made me "enter politics" and decided that, on the whole, it wasn't.

What I always felt after such encounters was there was no way I could turn anyone from Leave to Remain. I was more likely, on the whole, to persuade Remainers to vote Leave. When I canvassed for the Lib Dems in Vauxhall in 2017, Kate Hoey called Boris to complain. "Don't worry, Kate, old girl," my brother reassured her warmly. "Every person she knocks up is a surefire vote for you!"

· · ·

ON THIS, MY THIRD AND MOST FATEFUL TRIP TO BATH DUR-ing the campaign, I stood under the delicate white fretwork awning of the honey-stoned station, as instructed. The station clock stood at noon. A man who had been in my carriage slunk up to me. "I voted for you," he said. "You never!" I said. He took out his phone and showed me a photo of his postal vote, and there was a cross by my name on the ballot paper. I can't tell you how gratifying this was.

"What are you doing in Bath?" I said, thinking he might be a rare Chuka superfan or something, attending the Change UK rally because he believed in us.

"I'm having laser eye surgery," he said, darting off into town. I gazed after him with wet eyes. If someone votes for you, it's almost as good as when someone pays cold hard cash for your book.

The slate and the team—plus Elle Dormer, the press officer—soon arrived in force behind me off the same train, and we marched in a pack along the sleepy Avon and crossed a bridge right by Bath Cricket Club and Pavilion. As I trotted along, abreast with Crispin Hunt of Longpigs, I gave press interviews to straggling journos. Austrian and German TV. *Madame Figaro*. We crossed a bridge into a car park, and the emerald green of the cricket ground unrolled before us. The Change UK white-and-black-branded battlebus was parked up at a strange angle in the car park.

"Rachel! Stop!" a voice called.

I halted. John Crace of *The Guardian*—an angular streak—was running after me holding up his iPhone. "Can you stand in front of the bus?"

I posed in front of the bus.

Minutes later, Crace tweeted the picture: "Am in Bath with Rachel Johnson and a bus—what can go wrong?"

We skirted the boundary of the fifteen-pitch square, bordered by a picket fence with advertising hoardings for local light industry like lubricants and farm machinery. The town beyond the grass and river basked in the glorious sunshine and its own grandeur. I could see the TV crews setting up in front of the "pav." I wished I was coming to lie on a blanket beyond the boundary while leafing through the papers downing pints of Pimm's, but it was not to be.

A county cricketer in short shorts lay on a sort of gurney, receiving a groin massage from a physio. A groundsman was mowing the bowling-green lawn, making sure he turned and revved his engine right in front of the pavilion so all the interviews with

Change UK's top team by media crews from all over Europe had to pause and restart when he had gone to the other end of the pitch. He was definitely doing it on purpose. "Bloody Brexiteer," I said.

We did team photos on the boundary: the slate first in suits, no ties, Liz Sewell in a stripy jersey, me in my green dress. Then one with MPs, with Sarah Wollaston in the middle. Chuka seemed a bit flat, I thought. But I was sure he would perk up when everyone arrived and it all got going!

Inside the pavilion, eight lines of chairs had been arrayed facing a lectern. Our much-maligned signs with the Change UK logo (of black bars on a white background) that everyone on Twitter compared to a Tesco bar code were affixed to the wall behind the lectern, to provide a backdrop. Almost all the chairs were empty. That's okay, nothing is supposed to happen until 2:00 p.m., I told myself. John Crace of *The Guardian* tweeted yet another picture. "There are more candidates at the Bath rally than supporters!"

The room filled up; I shook hands and congratulated people on coming. "I like your university scarf," I said to one middle-aged male in striped maroon-and-navy varsity neckwear. "It's Jack Wills actually," he said. I had no idea what to say, even though I am in general *numera una assoluta* when it comes to small talk. I was new to this.

"We've got a lectern *and* a bus now!" said Joan Ryan, MP, beaming as if Christmas had come early. The MPs came and sat in a row behind the lectern: Joan Ryan, Sarah Wollaston, Chuka.

The party's high-ups must have dimly realised that the lobby, sketch writers, and international media wouldn't come to Bath on a school day to listen to a dozen bed-wettingly Europhile speeches from no-hopers back to back in a glorified shed. In the end, the high command narrowed it down to "only" seven (!) speakers: Sarah Wollaston, me, Ollie Middleton, Liz Sewell, Jim Godfrey, Chuka, and Joan Ryan, in that order.

As a warm-up before the main event there was the little video of the six South West candidates out and about on the stump, which Tim McCarron, Jo's brother, had made. It had been the whole point of several trips to Bristol. This was going to be played to razz people up for when we walked in, on a screen fixed for the occasion on the right-hand wall.

We mustered outside the pav, and someone hit play on the video. It was showtime.

We stood outside the pav peering in, waiting for our cue. It was obvious to all even outside that after only a minute the promo video of the candidates had freeze-framed. The pinwheel of doom was going round and round as the film buffered. The journalists were already tittering behind their hands at the frozen fuzzy screen in gleeful expectation of further fun and games at our expense.

It was by now five past two.

The video of the South West slate leafleting pensioners in cagoules in rainy Plymouth wasn't working on the side wall where nobody could see it anyway. We were shooed forward. I marched in with the others. Seconds after I took my seat to the left of Chuka Umunna, the Change UK banners with the black bar codes behind me, Sarah Wollaston introduced me as "one of the many, many fantastic candidates we are so proud of" and said how I was going to change our broken politics—please give a warm welcome to Rachel Johnson!

The crowd clapped politely. I knew that as far as the audience was concerned (1) I was Boris's sister; (2) I'd joined the Lib Dems; and (3) I took my top off on Sky News in a protest against Brexit (actually I didn't, it's too complicated to explain; I was wearing a flesh-coloured boob tube, but never mind that now, for some I am forever "that naked Remain lady," and whatever I say, someone asks me, "Taken your tits out on *The Pledge* recently?").

John Crace gave me the thumbs-up and winked.

I thanked Sarah and leapt to my feet. I was wearing trainers, and if I stood behind the new magic lectern, you couldn't see my face (I am five feet four on a good day), so I began unscrewing the mic so I could pace about dynamically, in a sleeves-rolled-up, new-health-secretary-visiting-NHS-hospital-ward way.

After a brief struggle, I got it off its stand and got going. I could see the top of Chuka Umunna's smooth, glossy brown head with its executive, power-shaved sides. As I spoke, it seemed to sink lower and lower into his chest. Sarah Wollaston gave me full-beam headlights of encouragement. John Crace and Henry Deedes stared at me without expression as if studying a disappointing laboratory experiment.

The actual members, or registered supporters, our rank and

Front page of the *Morning Star,* April 24, 2019.

file, sat solidly in their seats and glared at me, as if they'd dragged themselves off the sofa to hear me giving the motivational pep talk at the first Weight Watchers meeting after the summer, and it had better be *vaut le voyage*.

I didn't have notes. I shot from the hip. I told them about losing the Cornish vote with my cream tea tweet and being attacked by the *Morning Star* for having two AGAs (let it never be said that I don't know my audience). Important detail: I made it clear my two AGAs were *not in the same house*. I told them how I could not stand by and let the irrational surge of nationalism and populism drown out the European in all of us. I paid warm tribute to our MPs (I regarded this as my profoundly moving "Lessons in Courage" section).

I told them I was proud to be standing for a party where the MPs were so bold that they staked their careers on building a new sort of politics, where facts and experts mattered and they didn't deal in lies and they stood up to racism. My voice throbbed with conviction. I then shifted gear. I told the small crowd that it was a hard road as a newbie in a newbie party.

"You will be told that your party has not changed the weather. You are in the relegation zone compared to the Premier League of the Lib Dems and the Brexit Party," I said. "Twitter will mock your name, your message, your supporters, your poll ratings, your candidates; even the branding on your amazing new bus that you can see with its engine running outside will be compared to a Tesco bar code. You will pause so long when asked a question by a *Today* reporter that the station almost plays the emergency tape it has ready in case it falls off air. People will laugh and point and hand your leaflets back to you, and yes, I might have my arse handed to me on a plate by a triumphant Ann Widdecombe in Poole at the count on 26 May and you know what?

"This is just when you know you have to keep going. You are

annoying all the right people. You have to be there and stand up and be counted.

"I know one thing from my short career in politics," I continued. "As anyone who has tried to canvass in Plymouth on the coldest May bank holiday in history will confirm. A vote is earned, not owed. There is no such thing as a free vote. I know it's a big ask to go into an unwanted election calling for another, divisive referendum. It's a big ask. But these are dangerous times. We must show courage and conviction under fire. Vote Change UK on 23 May!"

People started to clap in the hope that I had finished.

"Oh yes," I said. "Sorry, I forgot! I forgot the only thing people really want to know is—sorry, the *two* things—first, what is Sunday lunch like in the Johnson family?"

I could sense I had the room with this. I would be a rich woman if I had a quid for everyone who asked what Sunday lunch was like and said how they would like to be a fly on the wall. Even heavenly Henry Deedes looked up. But I couldn't give them what they wanted. At family gatherings, we never talk about politics. Also, we don't have family Sunday lunch. We're not a Sunday roast type of family.

"And the other thing they want to know is, what did Boris say when you told him about standing against the referendum?"

I didn't actually answer these two questions.

"All I can tell you is—I am loving being part of the Change UK family! It's almost as dysfunctional as my own!" I finished with a flourish.

Then I realised that this would be the top line in the sketches ("Boris's sister compares useless party to her own dysfunctional family") unless I corrected myself.

"JOKE!" I screeched. "JOKE!"

All too soon it was the turn of Joan Ryan MP, who made a

long speech during which everyone could recover. In this she listed all the things that the EU had done for us. It was informational rather than inspirational. But at the end, she said, "And now, I want you all to do something for me."

We gazed at her. It was like circle time at school assembly. I was so relieved not to be at the lectern. I would have done anything for anybody at this point. "Look at your HANDS," she said. She held her hands in front of her, palms up, so we could follow her in a Simon Says way. Nobody stirred. Was this for real? I worried she was going to go round somehow checking whether we had all washed our hands after using the toilet.

"LOOK AT YOUR HANDS!" she commanded again (I kept hearing "hunds," so was even more confused).

Everyone put down their notebooks or iPhones. We all sat there staring down at our palms. Was she going to read them? I looked up, caught John Crace's eye, and looked away quickly.

"There's the answer!" she said in the voice of a vicar crying, "Christ is risen—Christ is risen indeed!" on Easter Sunday.

"The answer is in your HUNDS."

After a stunned pause, Chuka's press officer, Stuart—the one who had told me at the launch rally in Bristol that "nobody is your friend"—began clapping desperately.

There were no questions at the end, but that was because all the hacks were back on their phones and running for the exits. Something was breaking.

As I was making my way to the bar, where the man with the Jack Wills scarf was chatting up the lady behind the cheese scones on the counter, Stuart put an arm on my shoulder and steered me into a corner.

"Just thought you should know," he said.

"What?" I asked.

"One. You just conceded the election."

"No, I didn't!" I said.

"Yes, you did. You never, ever say you're going to lose. You've got to be more upbeat! More positive! But that's not it."

"What's happened?"

"Your brother's just announced that of course he's going to run to replace May. He'll be the next Tory leader. He's up north giving some speech to some insurers."

He let this sink in. If Al was running, he was a shoo-in. Which meant that I would be trying and failing to become an MEP while he was becoming prime minister.

I stumbled outside into the sunshine where the stoop and bleachers were lined with interviewers and crews. Chuka was doing an hour live with Theo Usherwood of LBC at a trestle table. I was due to chat to *Newsnight* and various other outlets as planned, but it was clear that the high-ups no longer regarded me as Change UK's secret weapon. I was a liability.

"Upbeat!" Stuart hissed in my ear as Stephen Smith of *Newsnight* approached first, with a cameraman and soundman.

"Don't answer their questions; just hammer our three core messages!" He then took up a position behind the cameraman. "You only have three questions," he said to each interviewer, and as I spoke, he made throat-cutting gestures.

Afterwards I went back inside to the bar, and a kindly woman who had witnessed the whole "rally" handed me a glass of water without being asked. "There you go, my lover," she said.

I found Stuart on the way out, as we were all going leafleting and canvassing (that is, going to sit in a Pret, eat jumbo chocolate chip cookies, and lick our wounds) with Sarah Wollaston afterwards.

"Don't worry," I said, as I posed for a few more photographs in my floral green wrap dress. "It may not have gone to plan today, but on Saturday," I promised, "it will all be different, as the *Times Mag* has done a big interview with me. Could be a game changer. A big win."

Stuart smiled for the first time. "Great," he said, and went off to find Chuka.

At the start of the campaign, a fine writer called Nigel Farndale had come to see me on Exmoor. We had sat by the fire, talking and talking, and gone for a walk. I had told him everything. I trusted him, even after he told me he'd voted Leave. I explained that to me Brexit was a midlife crisis event; we'd had a happy marriage with the EU. Like all marriages it had its ups and downs, it wasn't perfect, but we were throwing it away for something that wasn't worth it and trading the U.K. for a mess of pottage. I dimly remembered being a little frank about the party, perhaps too frank, but as it was almost flatlining in the polls, I was only being honest. Nigel had asked me about Jo, Boris, my father, my upbringing. I had tried to be discreet and disciplined, but in the end I always run my mouth.

There was one line I remembered that I prayed Nigel hadn't used. "I am the rat that jumps on the sinking ship," I'd said with a laugh as I put the kettle on and popped some tea cakes in the toaster. I had also done an extensive shoot to accompany the interview, astride the farm Land Rover in rugged locations, with several of the neighbour's blond Clumber spaniels as accessories. The interview was due to be published that Saturday.

That same evening, the Thursday, John Crace's sketch in *The Guardian* about the Bath rally was up. The headline: "Change UK Is Dying Before It Even Learned to Walk." It was even more savage than I expected. "Even the *Leftian* has abandoned Change UK," someone commented.

In the accompanying photographs, Chuka's head has sunk so low that it looked as if he were discreetly being sick into his own lap.

14

Bristol

DAYS TO ELECTION 6

As we entered the final week, there was no getting away from it. Every single wheel of the Change UK battlebus was coming off at once and spinning into the verge. I had conceded the election, and the "arse on a plate" line was repeated ad nauseam.

On the Friday before polling day I was on a train to Bristol, for two hour-long hustings back to back at the BBC. When I got to the BBC, the PM, Mrs. May, was also in the building, going through the motions of launching the Tory Euro campaign with just one reporter and one Tory MEP, Ashley Fox. In order to avoid any cross-contamination with her and Ann Widdecombe's large entourages, I was kettled in a dusty back room behind the studios as all the dressing rooms were taken up by far more important people.

"We'll come and get you soon," a floor manager said, and flipped on a light by the door so I didn't have to sit on my own in the dark. I sat having a Kit Kat and looking at my iPhone, trying to get my head around the main industries in the South West and how they would be affected by a deal or no deal, when a text came through. Actually, four texts in succession. All from my leader in all but name, Chuka.

The first said, "This is very dispiriting for our staff and candidates. Why say it this side of Thursday [that is, Election Day]?"

Say what? I went, my heart sinking.

The second was a link to the interview and spread with me by Nigel Farndale in the *Times Magazine*. I had been told it was going to be in the paper on Saturday, May 18—that is, the next day. But it was 3:00 p.m. on Friday. *The Times* had put it out ahead of schedule as they thought they had a story to tee up the next day's paper.

The third text was a screenshot of an extract from the interview:

"In 2017 I joined the Lib Dems just in time for them to flatline in the polls and I even managed to finish *Big Brother* off. I'm the format finisher. The rat that jumps on the sinking ship." She laughs. "And now I'm jumping on another sinking ship with Change UK. We hope it's not sinking but it's not riding the ocean waves the way Chuka (Umunna) and Heidi (Allen) and Anna (Soubry) thought it would."

Chuka's fourth text said, "This will be quoted straight back at me on *Marr* on Sunday. What should my reply be?"

I quickly read the interview, which had already generated a news story that, I noted, was being much RTd by the likes of Guido, Westmonster, and other mucho macho bloggers of SW1. The news story was headlined, "Rachel Johnson Has Sinking Feeling at Change UK," and the first par read, "Change UK has a bad name, a confused leadership structure and should have made a pact with other Remain parties, one of its leading candidates in the European elections next week has said."

The floor manager came and knocked on the door as I was sitting head in hands, thinking, *What have I done?* Did I really say those things? Of course, no getting away from the truth: I thought those things, and so did Chuka—everyone did—but could I have really said them out loud to a journalist? On the record? If I had, there was no doubt in my mind. I was not cut out for politics, and politics had cut me out in its turn.

In the first hustings I sat across a sofa from Ann Widdecombe and Ashley Fox, MEP, and the cameras started rolling. I have no idea what I said. None at all.

In the second hustings, I had to go into a little cupboard and stare into a camera set up on its own, as everyone else was in a studio in Falmouth. My phone, which I had put on the side as I sat in front of the round black eye of the camera, was buzzing like a wasp with angry and accusing texts from head office, Chuka, and others. I heard a disembodied voice in my ear.

"So, this show is sector-specific, and will be going out after *Marr* on BBC Cornwall," said a voice. "This is on fish and ag, and if we run out of fish and ag, we'll do some environmental impact stuff, beaches and pollution and suchlike."

"What?" I wailed. "Seriously? Nobody told me any of this!"

"Going to Rachel first in Bristol," I heard a different voice say, and then theme music.

I could only pray that no voters would be watching on Sunday (both filmed hustings were set to air after *The Andrew Marr Show* on different regional programmes on BBC West—that is, after Chuka's turn in the hot seat).

In the car taking me back to Bristol station, I composed and sent Chuka a text. It was a masterpiece of evasion and self-justification. "I know *The Times* wasn't 3,000 words of me hammering core messages but you know that's not how these things pan out," I wrote as the taxi lurched through Friday evening traffic. "Please try to think of it as a big piece of free publicity for Change UK in the *Times Mag* saying VOTE JOHNSON—that can't be a total fail," and on it went. But I knew that the horse had already bolted.

The party was over and so was my brilliant career in politics. It was a bit like being a parent. You are never praised for the hundreds of times you show up at the school play, healthy-eating assembly, pond-dipping expedition, all the things you do unnoticed every day from World Book Day to university graduation.* You are remembered only for the times you messed up, or you didn't come—or you put a single foot wrong.

Only the week before, for example, I'd been asked by the "head of stakeholder engagement" to speak at a fund-raiser on a boiling-hot May day.

The lunch had been held, for some reason, in the M basement restaurant in the Zig Zag Building on Victoria Street. I had turned up, said hello to everyone, said a few passionate words to shake down the donors over the starter, and then was chatting to my fellow candidate Gavin Esler about how, er, things were going when the man opposite leaned across the table and ticked me off for talking to Gavin Esler (full disclosure: I was negging about the fact that the three-course set lunch was a lordly £62— who on earth was paying?) rather than fluffing and flattering the other guests.

---

* When did graduation become a thing, incidentally? My parents didn't even take me to boarding school on my first day at Bryanston. My grandfather took me in the farm Land Rover, and when he dropped me off at my house, he didn't even cut the engine, as you had to open the bonnet and hit the starter motor with the spanner to get her going again, so I had to haul my trunk out of the back and go into the school on my own.

I hadn't been schooled like that since I was a teenager.

On the train to Taunton from Bristol I ate a banana stolen from a BBC Bristol fruit bowl and stared out the window. The train had halted at Worle. I was late and Ivo was waiting, sending me "Where are you?" texts every minute or so and updating me in real time as to his exact location at Taunton station and the exact location of the car as, whatever I do, I always manage to exit on the "wrong" side.

Chuka had not responded to my texts suggesting how he should respond to my Ratner moment. ("Every leader needs a Johnson ha-ha. . . . Rachel has many qualities but hasn't learned how to speak fluent politician yet." I'd sent him several "lines" in my guilt and panic.) His silence was crushing.

"I've been everywhere else in the South West and got the T-shirt, so why not give Worle a whirl?" I said out loud in the crowded carriage of the stopping train.

I got through Saturday and people sending me texts teasing me about my *Times* interview. On Sunday, I bravely removed the tartan blanket that shrouds the TV in our farmhouse on Exmoor to watch *The Andrew Marr Show*. Andrew Marr hunched over his chair. Chuka lolled in his, smooth-skinned, luminous, his skull gleaming under the lights; magnificent. First question from Marr.

"Your lead candidate in the South West, Rachel Johnson, says you have a terrible name, a terrible leadership structure, and you failed to make a pact with the other Remain parties so you will split the Remain vote in next Thursday's European elections." I closed my eyes in pain. "She has likened herself to a rat that has jumped onto a sinking ship. What do you say to that?"

I waited for Chuka to deliver one of the many rebuttal lines I had sent him.

"You should hear what she says to me about Boris," he said, smiling.

I'd met Chuka only once, and as even my many detractors would admit, I am blindly loyal to all my brothers in public and in private.

Revenge in politics is clearly a dish best eaten straightaway!

Thick of It Moment 8: My postal vote arrived. I read the accompanying leaflet carefully. I put a cross by my own name, thinking, "This is the first and only time I will ever vote for myself," and posted it. This meant driving down the two-mile track to the postbox on the nearest tarmac road and back, a round-trip of about half an hour. I waited to feel something. I felt nothing.

When I got home, I found the counterpart of the form, the signature and date of birth declaration, that you HAVE to return with the ballot paper, on my desk.

My vote was invalid without it.

I almost burst into tears.

I was so hopeless I couldn't even get ME to vote for me!

. . .

LATER, I WAS GETTING THE FLAT-IRON CHICKEN WITH "coronation dressing" from M&S out of the AGA for supper, and my mobile started ringing. Calls were coming in from the Change UK leaders. I had long talks with Sarah Wollaston and Heidi Allen. I sat on the doorstep to catch the sun dipping over the valley, the swifts dipping and the bluebells turning from blue to violet as we spoke. Heidi told me that the leadership was at sixes and sevens. Half were talking to the Lib Dems. The party would split. Chris Leslie and Anna Soubry would be left in a rump Change UK.

But before all that happened, there was an almighty row as

we went into polling day. Heidi Allen and Sarah Wollaston knew it was game over, but—like a family sitting around a patient on his deathbed—they wanted us to be able to do some good before we went; she wanted us to donate our organs to other Remain parties. As we were polling at 3 per cent, Heidi wanted to concede. She wanted to tell everyone to vote not for us but for the Remain party in the region that had the best chance of returning a candidate. Heidi wanted to put country before party. She wanted people's votes to count.

I heard her out. I understood.

"But the problem is my name is on the ballot paper," I said. "Postal votes have been sent out and returned." I didn't see how the party could concede the election and ask our supporters to vote for other pro-Remain parties when all our faces were on all the tea towels.

I was getting daily texts from Remainiacs like Anatole Kaletsky, the economist and adviser to George Soros, and Hugo Dixon from the People's Vote. Hugo had been at Ashdown House prep school with us, and like many of Boris's oldest friends he is an out-and-out pro-European activist. I have no idea if those two things are related. All Hugo's texts to me always start "darling," however unpleasant the message he is trying to impart.

"Darling: you can't win in the south west. But you could deny the Lib Dems a second seat there—or the Greens their only MEP. Have you thought of saying it might be best to vote for one of them instead?"

Anatole Kaletsky wrote asking me to concede and hand my votes to the Lib Dems: "You could be the Joan of Arc of Remain."

I replied, "But Anna Soubry is the Jeanne d'Arc of Remain."

I left Exmoor on Sunday night to return to London. In the grid, I had media throughout Monday and Tuesday: Adam

Boulton, *Politics Live,* an interview on *PM,* an hour on LBC with Eddie Mair. Wednesday was Gibraltar (for reasons I don't understand, Gib is part of the South West region). Thursday was Election Day.

Elle Dormer, the refugee from Tory Central Office, called me on the train back on Sunday night. Her last communication to me was a WhatsApp that said, "A lot of almost deliberately unhelpful comments, Rachel. Office feeling pretty pissed at you."

Anyone who ends a text or WhatsApp with a full stop isn't passive-aggressive. They are active aggressive. I took Elle's call in the train corridor, but the signal kept breaking up and the loo doors kept opening and closing; it was impossible to have a meaningful exchange, and we gave up.

Minutes later I received a careful and kindly message from Elle. It said that the party wanted its MP leaders to take on my national media bids, so Soubs would do most of it and the bits Soubs couldn't do, Gavin Esler would do, such as LBC. I accepted this.

"That way you can focus on Gibraltar and local/regional stuff," Elle said, but we both knew that I was being ghosted by the party after I had Ratnered them out in *The Times.*

15

Gibraltar

DAY TO ELECTION 1

On the eve of battle, May 22, I got up at 4:00 a.m. to catch the BA flight to Gibraltar. The plane seemed to be flying straight into the Rock (another metaphor for Brexit) and then straight into the sea but at the last minute dropped onto a short runway on the isthmus that—my eyes boggled as I took this in—bisected the main road and pedestrian thoroughfare into town. The road had to be closed every time a plane took off or landed.

The hair dryer heat, the cloudless zinging blue sky, did not sync one bit with the stale Englishness of the place. The airport is owned by the Ministry of Defence and has a NAAFI canteen feel to it, and the first sign to greet arrivals informs them the Rotary Club meets every Tuesday at the Rock Hotel at 7:15 p.m.

My old nanny Mary Kidd, who works in Gib for a betting company, picked me up and drove me. Our first stop was Number 6, the HQ of HM's government and the office of the chief minister, Fabian Picardo. Travelling with Mary (formerly Nanny Kidd) was a bit Jacob Rees-Moggy, but I needed her and hoped it might lead to a charming nib in the *Daily Mail* and go a small way towards making up for the weekend's media car crash. As Mary drove (her car had G.B. plates), I inspected the beflagged pubs, the bunting-decked streets, and Great Britain tourist shops selling Union Jack mugs and cast-iron model steam trains.

The government building was a gracious affair with a portico and palm trees outside. Within, a seating area with a wide-screen TV was showing the BBC, and the words "Her Majesty's Government" in huge gold letters were stencilled on the wall. As my brother was about to become PM, Picardo, quite understandably, didn't want to talk about Change UK, or me, but whether Gibraltar—which voted 99 per cent to remain—would be thrown to the four winds by the Brits as a "bargaining chip" to buy off the Spanish over fishing rights in any future trade deal. We talked through Yellowhammer base-case scenarios (Yellowhammer was the code name used by the Treasury for the civil contingency planning for leaving the EU without a withdrawal agreement—that is, a no-deal withdrawal). I had been processed into Gib in minutes, but after a no-deal Brexit, as we weren't in Schengen, that could be more like four hours.

Fabian was of the view that the only way to avert no deal (and gridlock in Gibraltar) was to "flush Theresa May's withdrawal agreement down the legal loo" and Revoke; only revoking Article 50 would, he said, buy more time and seize control of the agenda and timetable from the EU to renegotiate. I gave him my brother's mobile number and left him. I knew that Revoke was the last thing Al would do as PM, let alone the first. We did the grip and grin by his front door, next to a wire sculpture of a World War I soldier with his head bowed over his bayonet.

Total cost of day trip: £675.

Total number of votes cast for Change UK in Gibraltar the following day: 77.

Cost-per-vote ratio: more than £8.

Takeaway from the exercise?

A vote is not earned. Or even owed. In my case it is paid for!

Worth it? Undoubtedly. As my mother told me when I was whining about being tired and bored by housework and motherhood, "No experience is ever wasted."

. . .

I FLEW BACK FROM GIB INTO A MINOR FIRESTORM.

Heidi Allen had gone on *Channel 4 News* that evening, unaware that her loyal colleague Soubs had booby-trapped her appearance by tipping off the interviewer (Cathy Newman) that she (Heidi) wanted to concede the election and tell Remainers to vote for other parties and not us. When Cathy Newman popped a preloaded leading question about this, Heidi burst into tears. They had to stop and start the interview all over again. "All we have left is our integrity," Heidi tearfully concluded her eve-of-battle interview.

I spoke to Chris Leslie, who had called to discuss with me, as a lead candidate, whether Allen should chuck in the towel and whether we should concede. We agreed we couldn't.

"Poor Heidi darling, she's had a wobble," he said.

I could hardly blame her. My line about being a rat jumping on a sinking ship was being quoted extensively to each of them, like a catechism, whenever they did media. The center of the center party had not held. The tensions in the group had erupted like a whale breaching the surface of an already roiling sea and was sinking the party.

"To have your leader saying in the final moments of the campaign don't vote for my party is devastating and extremely foolish," said Anna Soubry.

Gavin Shuker, MP, admitted, "This is not coming back."

The polls had us between 3 per cent and 0 per cent, Tories

and Labour down, Greens and Lib Dems and Brexit up. In some polls, therefore, nobody asked was planning on voting for us. I felt as if I were living through an extinction-level event. Nobody in my family dared mention what I was doing at all on Election Day.

The *famiglia* Johnson WhatsApp group continued to celebrate birthdays religiously but never mentioned politics or current affairs. Nobody even said, "Good luck, Rake," to me, as I went into my first-ever national election; it was that bad.

The polls opened in less than twelve hours.

▬▬▬▬▬▬

16

Poole

DAYS AFTER THE ELECTION 3

In the afternoon, Ivo and I drove to Poole for the results (as they were European elections, over twenty-eight countries, the vote was declared on the Sunday after polling day). We lay down on the tiny bed in our tiny room in the Thistle Hotel (£139!), overlooking the seafront. There was no space on the floor even for our bags. "Let's go to the pub," I said. "We've got at least seven hours before all this is over and normal life can resume."

The Poole Arms, a gabled, green-tiled hostelry that boasted it was the oldest pub on the quay, was yards away and still serving Poole oysters, scallops, and crab salad, which seemed like an everyday miracle as it was after 2:00 p.m. We sat side by side in the snug and ordered more buttered bread. Matt Hooberman, number five of the slate, joined us. After a few more halves of local ale we drove off around sleepy Poole to the count, which was being held in the Lighthouse Arts Centre in the middle of town.

Interesting data point: it is the largest arts center in the U.K. outside London. When I googled it, someone had complained,

"The cinema is comfortable but the film started twenty minutes late and the snack store was closed."

I was given a yellow lanyard saying "count pass" and "CANDIDATE" on it by the council officer at the entry. Upstairs, outside the hall, the first person I recognised was the Sargon of Akkad, the Brexit Party YouTuber candidate, who looked pleasant enough in a navy suit, standing by the bar (which, like the snack store, was closed).

I went into the 669-seat theatre. There was a low, purposeful hum and a sound of papers flicking and rubber bands snapping. Hands were a blur of motion, licking fingers, sorting, bundling. The tellers—all volunteers, all unpaid—were counting our votes and speaking little in quiet voices. Here was democracy in action, and I can't deny, it was strangely moving. So many people had given up their Sundays for this.

I remembered what my friend Eddy (a.k.a. Lord Faulks, and a justice minister under Michael Gove) once said to me about our elections. He described to me "the extraordinary privilege" of being able to vote in secret, knowing that you were electing members of Parliament. "The act of voting has given rise to such controversy and been the subject of violent dispute and corruption all over the world. And yet in this country we abide by the result, and everyone over a certain age can vote knowing there will be no adverse consequences and that their vote will count. Not something to be taken for granted."

I didn't take it for granted. I felt a surge of humbled gratitude, as you do when an NHS registrar saves you and your as-yet-unborn baby's life in the middle of the night, or a pilot lands you safely in a storm.

Above the stage there was a sign saying "Collations" as if there were a smorgasbord of cold meats beneath. At rapid intervals, tellers came up and placed bundles of votes in sheaves of a hundred in colour-coded piles onstage. The biggest piles by far were for the Brexit Party. Then the Lib Dems. Then the Greens. Then the Tories. Then Labour. And Change UK?

Change UK was nowhere, but it felt like a handicapped team coming last in a rugby tournament against an able-bodied pack that weighed three times as much. It was the taking part that mattered. I wandered round the tables. We had some votes, but on some tables our putty-coloured bundles were only just more plentiful than the spoilt ballots. Someone had just scrawled, "BREXIT BREXIT BREXIT," on their ballot paper. Another read, "NONE OF YOU ARE GOOD ENOUGH!" I was amazed that day to see any ballot papers with a cross next to my name. It seemed astonishing. People had actually voted—and for me. What a turn-up.

We didn't hang around. At seven, we all met for a last pizza supper on the quay. Matt, Crispin, Liz, Jo the organiser, Jim, Sarah Wollaston, and all their "partners." It was a funereal affair. I said a few words, thanking them. Liz gave everyone a photocard of all of us together in Totnes at the beginning, before hope had been utterly extinguished. Sarah advised us that we didn't really need to go to the declaration—that is, the arse-plating ceremony at the town hall later. "Just turn up to show your faces, shake hands, avoid media interviews"—Sarah tried not to look at me—"then home to a stiff drink and bed!"

I also apologised to them all for the *Times* interview. To their credit, none had taken me to task for it. "Look, when I worked for Labour, everyone had media training, which was all about making sure you never said anything interesting that a newspaper could use against you," said Matthew Hooberman. "You have just not learned that skill."

We left the restaurant for the count.

We had started, and therefore we would finish.

We drove in convoy to the town hall. It was by now dark and cold. TV vans—Sky, the BBC—were mobilised outside in the pitchy Dorset night to beam the results of the European elections 2019 to the waiting world. We got our teas and Kit Kats and settled round a table as far away from the Brexit Party and UKIP tables as possible. Television screens showed the results programmes hosted by Emily Maitlis, Huw Edwards, and so on.

As time passed, photocopied spreadsheets from the local counting areas came in. Runners handed them round. These were the results in the various regions. They were much pored over, with much cheering from the Brexit table presided over by Ann Widdecombe in a purple and indigo tiered and ruffled frock, a British Battleaxe Blue jacket with a splashy pale blue Brexit Party rosette as a boutonniere.

A typical A4 spreadsheet for the South West region would have the following information:

CORNWALL

Total electorate: 424,255
Total papers verified: 175,475
Change UK the Independent Group: 4,191
Conservative and Unionist Party: 13,486
English Democrats: 924
Green Party: 31,544
Labour: 10,782
Liberal Democrats: 34,845
The Brexit Party: 71,681
UKIP: 6,209

As we had been to the count, our expectations had been very much managed. As the sheets poured out, all we could hope for was that we would, please God, at least get more votes than UKIP. But things didn't look good. In Bristol City, where I had stumped and leafleted every week of the campaign, we congealed only 3,258 votes. Ten minutes into the BBC's coverage I had been referred to as "Boris Johnson's sister" by Huw Edwards and not by my own name.

For the actual declaration, we had to move upstairs to an even smaller room. As there were so many candidates, it was agreed that only the first three winning MEPs would give speeches. We clustered alongside a returning officer and in front of the press. Then, at midnight, the Brexit Party was declared the outright winner with the first three seats. The Lib Dems got two. The Greens got one.

Ann Widdecombe flung her arms wide in ecstasy and turned her white throat to the strip lighting and closed her eyes, as if spread-eagled on some holy cross. We had a vote share of 3.4 per cent across the board. We did beat UKIP, but only just. SS *Change UK,* having steamed out of harbour at 17 per cent, made it into port, as my husband observed, "more like Géricault's *Raft of the Medusa.*" The Change UK share in the South West, I was dispirited to note, was 2.7 per cent.

The slate peeled off. We had failed. Not a single Change UK MEP had been elected. Thousands of miles and thousands of pounds and thousands of hours of wasted breath had been spent chasing not a single seat. "We helped smash up the two-party system tonight," said Matt, who always takes the long view, as he steered the Sargon of Akkad away from live vlogging our weary table as the Brexit Party claque whooped every time they won a bit of the South West.

"It had to be done."

. . .

I SAID GOODBYE TO THE SLATE, WHO WENT BACK TO THEIR hotel rooms, and stayed in the town hall to deliver the interviews I'd promised to various outlets: BBC, Sky, LBC, and such. Ivo sat impatiently in the passage outside, sending me texts telling me to hurry up, waiting for me to emerge a free woman so we could go back to our room in the Thistle and resume normal life.

"As the cleaners looked at their watches in the foyer, you conducted a series of interviews into the early hours with Points West and Wiltshire Radio," he complained later as we lay in the dark trying to sleep, "no doubt on the principle that if you're out of votes, give them quotes."

In the end the party received almost 600,000 votes across the region, which was not nothing. The two main parties, meanwhile, imploded, and Theresa May resigned the next day. Nobody was that fixated on the fact that Change UK hadn't won a single seat. In politics, you learn how to recognise these small mercies, and also that someone else is always having an even shittier day or night than you.

Text from George Osborne: "My parents voted for Change" (the former chancellor did not disclose whom he voted for).

Text from my friend the Remain campaigner, novelist, and journalist Henry Porter: "Tough few weeks. Always the bravest thing to do is to fight a battle you expect to lose. That takes guts."

Thick of It Moment 9: On polling day, Change UK spent the lion's share of its total social media budget on a Facebook ad to put out a message saying, "Campaign for the UK to remain within the UK."

As Al cheerily observed when I sent the story to my brothers, "Well, that's one campaign promise delivered!"

. . .

HENRY PORTER'S TEXT MADE ME REMEMBER MY FIRST POLIT-
ical campaign. Bear with me.

Before Jo was even born, and we moved to Primrose Hill, I
lived with Leo, Al, and my mother for a year in a small cottage
in our Exmoor river valley (how green is my valley? Greener
than Greta Thunberg. It never stops raining). The cottage had
only two bedrooms: a main bedroom for my parents, with Leo
and I squashed into a bunk room next door. Al slept under the
eaves in a Toblerone section of the attic, from which he could
squint out at a shed built by the previous owner of the cottage,
a Mr. Cole, which contained male essentials such as lawn mower,
weed killer, tools, and workbench. The shed smelt so strongly
that even now I can summon the rusty, oily tang to my nostrils.

We slept in it whenever visitors came to stay (as the farm is
five hours from anywhere, nobody came for just one night). In
preparation for fine company my mother would lay out three
camp beds in a row for me, Leo, and Al in the shed, which
she would dress with a sleeping bag and pillow. At bedtime we
would trot the twenty yards to the shed in the dark in bare feet
and our pj's and try to go to sleep in the pitchy blackness.

In order to keep us in the shed in the morning without waking
the grown-ups in the cottage, my mother would leave midnight
snacks for us to eat as a first breakfast. These were invariably
disgusting: a soggy Ryvita with cheese, or a couple of digestives
she had tried to crisp up in the Rayburn.

To recap, there were three camp beds: an orange one, a green
army one, and a blue one, all equally uncomfortable. It was
agreed we would rotate so nobody had to sleep on the same
one twice in a row. One night in the shed, Leo, my younger
brother by two years, peed on the orange bed in the night. Fair

play to him—he couldn't find the sliding door to open it and go out. He was tiny. In the morning the sweet, rotting smell of urine permeated the shed.

It was my turn to sleep in the orange bed that night. I therefore began making the case that as Leo had peed on the orange bed, Leo should sleep in it for another night. The others—Leo and Al—made the point that even though Leo *had* wet the bed, it was still my turn to sleep in it. Rules were rules.

I made the point that this was unfair.

The arguments boiled over. We screamed. We argued passionately. It was the letter versus the spirit of the law. We painted slogans on the shed wall. Mine read, "Leo for the Orange Bed!" Al wrote, "Rake for the Orange Bed," in blue poster paint on the bare boards of the shed. He wrote, "Boo to Grown Ups," underneath, for good measure, a graffito that will go down in history as his first political slogan—an early precursor, some might say, to the populist rallying cries of "Get Brexit Done!" and "Make America Great Again!"

The rows went on and on. They became violent. We were so engrossed in the arguments that raged back and forth that we did not leave the shed apart from to go into the cottage for meals.

Night fell. I was sticking to my guns, but as we entered the "playroom" (my mother's preferred euphemism for the shed), my argument that Leo had to sleep in the bed for a second consecutive night had not prevailed. Reader, my mother and my brothers ganged up on me.

I slept in the orange bed that night. And as I went back to my drear room in the Thistle, I felt I slept in it again.

I had lost a fight—some might argue, with my own brother—I had never expected to win. But I had at least carried on fighting until the end, and I had gone down with the ship with my head high. Change UK didn't fight to win the European parliamentary elections, and oh, boy, we succeeded in that aim.

As I checked out of the Thistle Hotel, I realised I'd been charged £2.50 for my early morning tea as well as £139 for the room, and it was only then that I almost burst into tears at the unfairness of it all.

We hightailed it out of Poole, and we didn't stop to have breakfast until I was out of my formerly prospective constituency and in Winchester (we went to somewhere called Cafe Monde. Trip Advisor review: "My friend had a baked potato which also was very nice although beware any filling is charged extra"). I ordered for some reason the "full vegetarian English breakfast."

And then my phone buzzed. A text from my youngest son, Oliver. Hardly anyone in my family had acknowledged the fact I was standing for a national election as, let's face it, when you have two brothers in Westminster, one of whom is about to become PM by acclamation, nobody pays the slightest attention to what you do, or don't do. "So proud of you, Mum. You are really the best mum a son could ask for."

The tears dripped into my Linda McCartney vegan sausages. I sat opposite Ivo while he read *The Times* on his iPad and worked his way through his plate and I tapped out a loving answer to my son's text. As I did, the thought occurred. Just as my brother had achieved his lifetime ambition, I had also achieved mine. He was World King. (At a primary school in Milton Keynes in October, a little boy in school uniform asked him as he sat at a tiny chair, "You run the world, don't you?" and an expression of gleeful triumph I knew only too well flickered across his face.) I was a wife and mother. We had both done it.

Okay, I couldn't even be elected to anything, while my brother was being wafted ever closer to Number 10 on the zephyrs of

Alexander Boris with Rachel, holding Charlotte Millicent, and Ludo, in the garden in Notting Hill, 1994.

populism and anti-EU nationalism. But the consolations of my own comparative mediocrity felt sweet. My children loved me. My marriage was intact. Wasn't that all that mattered?

I flicked to Instagram.

"You got HUMPED," someone had written, with a line of crying laughing emoji and exclamation marks. I put my phone down.

"Can I ask you something?" asked Ivo.

"Let me order another coffee first," I said. Ivo spoke.

"As it is well known that this selfless tradition of service courses through the Johnson bloodstream and is buried deep in their DNA . . ."

I barked to show I knew he was being ironic.

He looked over his full piggy English plate. "Will you therefore—ahahaha—allow your name to go forward again?"

"What?" I spluttered.

People say politics is an addiction, but I felt inoculated by the experience. I remember arriving at St. Mary's, Paddington, to give birth to Charlotte Millicent fourteen months after I had crawled out of the labour ward with Ludo, and even the Irish midwives were shocked at my early return and asked, "Back so soon, Mrs. Dawnay?"

I wanted five babies, but on the morning of May 24, 2019, I felt that one election was more than enough.

"No," I said, explaining that standing for election and losing was not like childbirth. You never forget the pain. And you don't get a lovely baby at the end of it.

"Thank Christ," he replied, and asked for more toast.

Part Three

17

"Sister of the PM"

THE EUROPEAN ELECTIONS WERE THE END OF MAY, IN every sense.

A few short weeks later, in June 2019, it was clear that the country—the 160,000-strong Tory membership at any rate—was about to consummate its antique crush. People interviewed on politics shows or in marquees on College Green said things like "Only Boris can stop Boris now."

"The only thing that can stop him is if he killed someone," bro Jo said. Then corrected himself with care. "The only thing that can stop him is if it was *found out* he had killed someone."

My husband took to chanting as the day of destiny approached, "You are sister of the future prime minister," with a dark frown. Shit was getting real. Ivo is an out-and-out gloomster Remainiac, much given to trolling his brother-in-law from the sofa on Twitter.

It slightly made me long for the old days when I was "Stanley's daughter" or, even better, Ludo, Milly, or Oliver's mummy. About ten years ago, I was giving a talk at an *Oldie* lunch at Simpson's. The compère told the three hundred or so elegant guests powdered and prinked in their London best, "And

Rachel Johnson needs no introduction! Our next distinguished speaker is the editor of *The Lady* and"—nobody can ever resist the name drop, the association, even if they get it wrong—"the brother of Boris!"

Ivo is known as "the husband of the sister of Boris." Ivo's older brother Jamie says he is sometimes introduced—he lives in the remote Borders of Scotland, is a local laird, and has devoted some of his retirement to the impeccable restoration of the Biggar Museum—as the "brother of the brother-in-law of the PM."

"It's okay," Ivo said when I apologised to him about all of the above. "You are the sister of the future prime minister. Then you will be known as sister of the prime minister, and then he'll do a few months, get his house colours. And one day, it will be over, and we can all have our lives back."

He paused to mark the end of something that had not even begun yet. "And then, of course, you will be known as the sister of the former prime minister."

.   .   .

FOR THE TORY "CORONATION" OF ITS NEW LEADER, I MET my son Ludo at the Greggs concession in Westminster tube station. We were going together to witness the last stop on the line for my brother's jet-propelled ambition: Downing Street.

It was fully expected that Ludo's uncle had crushed Jeremy Hunt, the foreign secretary, in the party members' vote to become the next leader of the Conservative and Unionist Party, a role that handily came with prime minister and first lord of the treasury attached. It was a foregone conclusion, but his anointment with the precious secret oils of leadership amid a haze of blue-tinted wonder and joy still had to take place in front of the world's stunned gaze.

An hour earlier that day, I had played tennis with brother Jo.

We had to mop ourselves down afterwards; it was the hottest July day on record. Jo had tried to discourage me from coming. "It's a party event," he'd said, and shot down to change out of his shorts into his heavy black Levi's and navy serge jacket. When I queried the outfit (I'd seen someone on Twitter saying, "101 degrees in London and Boris in Downing St., we really are entering Hell"), he said it was his bicycling gear.

"We can't all go en masse," he said, worrying. "It's too Trumpy."

As *The New York Times* had already written that the Johnson family occupied "an amorphous space somewhere between the Kennedys and the Kardashians," I could hardly disagree, but it was a moment in history, and I wanted to be there. I acknowledge that I am compelled to insert myself in the narrative, like some latter-day Zelig, but I also went for another reason. If I went, even though people would say, "But she's a Lib Dem," and "What's that reject from Cringe UK doing here?," it would prove something. I was not sure what.

Johnson children with mother Charlotte, Mount Desert Island, Maine, 1980. *Left to right:* Leo, Alexander, Jo, Charlotte, Rachel.

I hoped it might suggest that if you could unite a family divided by politics, you could unite a country. That was the thought anyway as I WhatsApped my brothers from the changing room at the tennis club. "I'm coming with Ludo. After all, it's not every day you get to see Jeremy Hunt become PM!" (That was a joke. We all knew what fate had in store.)

On the Circle line from Notting Hill to Westminster, a man with a suitcase came and sat next to me. "Sorry. Are you who I think you are?" he asked.

"Probably," I admitted. There followed a long discussion about the options my brother faced as he assumed the highest office in the land. They were all bad.

There was no parliamentary majority for the deal. The EU was refusing to budge on the backstop. There was no parliamentary majority for no deal. There was no parliamentary majority, period. There was no majority in the country, either.

And the only way to get a majority would be to call a general election, but nobody in their right mind would do that before you'd got Brexit in the bag. Boris wouldn't have another referendum. Even I believed by that stage in the dispiriting argument that another referendum would solve nothing, even if thresholds, and a supermajority, were applied this time, and it was as much as sixty to forty for Remain. I subscribed, in the end, to President François Mitterrand's line that a referendum was too many people voting on a question that hasn't been asked. Even if the poll was a three-way one with No Deal, Deal, and Remain on the ballot paper, it would still leave the country split.

I could see no possible resolution in sight. Except a deal.

As the tube train travelled to Westminster in the infernal heat, I felt as if the country were trapped underground in a burning basement and the Brexit ultras in the Tory party were bolting the fire doors from the inside. How could anyone provide an escape when the plan seemed to be to push heavy items of furniture against every available fire door of the flaming house? It all seemed to prove something that Peter Mandelson said once that I thought sounded mad but as time passed made more and more sense.

Brexit will destroy Brexit. (The exact quotation, for political nerds, is "Brexit may even destroy Brexit with all its emerging contradictions, complexity, costs, and divisions," said at a Centre for European Reform event in November 2017.)

Ludo stood by the Greggs as arranged. Americano for me in his hand. Suit, no tie. My heart flipped when I saw him. "This is it, Mum," he said. "Your brother and my uncle is about to become PM."

We left Westminster and I pointed up to the London Transport sign denoting the Downing Street exit in silence. "It is completely surreal that tomorrow Al will, barring an act of God, be entering that shiny black front door and standing at that lectern and doing the vision thing," I said as we wove our way through the overheated throng of spads, tourists, policemen. I could write it in my head already.

Under his Augustan reign, which he would govern like a blond, overexcited crossbreed Churchill and Pericles puppy, there would be no talk of addressing the burning injustices of an unequal society. It would be all can-do optimism, a brighter future, longer bridges, even more buses and bikes and bigger breasts as his new Jerusalem would be built here. It would be time to let the sunshine in.

"Surreal," Ludo agreed. There was no other word for it.

As we approached the QEII Centre, the telly crews and demos and crowds—including a full-dress Morris-dancing protest with men in hose jangling bells and women covered with leaves so they looked like walking trees out of an am-dram production of *A Midsummer Night's Dream*—were already in full swing. I dumped my Greggs Americano by a lamppost as antiterrorism measures have washed Westminster clean of bins.

Two security guards manned a barrier. The press and baying mob and banner-waving protesters were penned across the road. "Can I help?" one asked. I had to do it. I had to say it. If you don't use it, you lose it.

"I'm Boris Johnson's sister, and this is my son," I muttered.

The red sea parted, and the first person to greet me in the milling hall was Al's long-serving secretary from *The Spectator,* who had followed him to city hall and Westminster, Ann Sindall, a.k.a. "the Sindall and End-all." She comes from Yorkshire and does not suffer fools. We have had our run-ins in the past, but Ann is a member of the family and I love her.

"I can't believe you've come to show your face here, Rachel," she said, her face darkening. (Ann is a woman who believes that sisters should stand by their brothers and not betray them by disagreeing with their politics publicly. The surrendered part of me partly agrees with her.)

"Thank you for your support, Ann," I said, kissing her.

I hit the coffee bar. When the appointed hour came, we filed in. We were assigned four seats abreast in the second row. I sat with Ludo, Jo, and my father. We chatted with the crowd. It was like a cocktail party crossed with a blue-chip jobs fair as the hopefuls milled around in their executive best. I noted that Gavin Williamson was shrimpier and pinker in the flesh. I poked Jo and pointed to a sturdy man I recognised from somewhere.

"Kit Malthouse," he said. "Known as Shit Brickhouse."

The entire cabinet or wannabe cabinet was there, flicking their hair, scrubbed up, including all those super-keen to help solve the "woman problem" in politics by their own promotions to cabinet: Liz Truss, Amber Rudd, Penny Mordaunt, Priti Patel, Theresa Villiers. I hugged Priti and whispered, "Hashtag HasToBeHunt" to her. She giggled, then checked herself. "Pack it in, Rachel," she said. "Not today!"

Sir Edward Lister, who'd served as Boris's chief of staff in city hall, was sitting just in front of me. He twisted round in his seat to chat. "He's got a hundred days to do it," he said. I presumed that was because there were exactly a hundred days between taking office and the hard stop of Hallowe'en, after which the U.K. would leave the EU, do or die.

"And we all know what happened a hundred days after Napoleon returned from Elba," Lister went on. Did we? "Waterloo," Sir Eddie said. That meant one thing. My bro had a hundred days to deliver Brexit, or it was curtains.

After what felt like hours (I had to go out to Pret for supplies and sustenance at least one more time), Brandon Lewis, the chairman of the party, came onstage with a cosy Tory matron who was the returning-officer-type figure. Johnson and Hunt, the two leadership hopefuls, came in from stage right and sat bang in front of me. I snapped a picture of their backs on my iPhone. The results were read out of the magic envelope.

In the TV footage of the event, I am staring at Jeremy Hunt's left ear (he came with his mum and his wife, who sat holding hands) as it is announced that my brother had won almost twice as many votes as the foreign secretary. I start slowly clapping, then rise to my feet to join in the standing ovation.

It was done. It had happened.

The thing that he said was as likely as being "reincarnated as an olive, locked in a disused fridge, and decapitated by a flying Frisbee" had come to pass. It had taken only half a century since my brother had first articulated his ambition, but the following day the die was cast. He would become the fifty-fifth PM of the U.K., aged fifty-five.

The president of the United States responded to the news by comparing my brother to him, which of course was his highest compliment, and welcomed the new "Britain Trump" on the world stage.

I got into hot water for going, of course. I had to tell some friends and family that I didn't go because I had a sudden conversion to a clean, pure Brexit.

I will always think Brexit is a stupid idea. There was no deal better than the one we had already. We were out of Schengen; out of the euro—that is, the monetary union; we had opt-outs on workers' rights, justice, home affairs; we had our rebate, our seat at the table, and in Brussels, if you didn't have your seat at the table, you were on the menu. We already had our cake and had been eating it for decades. The Common Agricultural Policy needed root-and-branch reform, I agree, but basically Brexit was taking back control of things we never lost to lose control of things we currently had. It was declaring economic war on ourselves.

But this did not stop me supporting him as a brother on the biggest day of his life.

Tweet of the Day: Robert Peston tweets a picture of me looking pensively thunderstruck. "What your sister thinks when you become PM." Someone replied, "Why is nobody tweeting speech bubbles of what Rachel Johnson is really thinking?"

· · ·

THE NEXT DAY, THERESA MAY LEFT DOWNING STREET FOR her last audience with the Queen, and her fourteenth PM, who had written a best-selling book about his hero Churchill, Her

Majesty's first PM, went to kiss her hand and be asked by the sovereign to form a government.

I was watching on TV. When my brother's motorcade was blocked in the Mall by climate-change protesters, I took advantage of the hiatus to text Peter Morgan, who wrote *The Crown,* as well as *The Queen* and *The Audience.* "Why don't you write a play about the hour or so that the country doesn't have a PM . . . does someone else like the cabinet secretary get custody of the nuclear codes . . . written from within Downing Street between handovers?"

There must surely be a play in it. A script that charted the ungoverned moments in British history when you can't cry "the king is dead" and in the next breath "long live the king," because for an hour or so there isn't one. I've always believed that the way we can sit and watch a five-set tennis match inside a dark room for hours on end on a hot summer's day is a testament not to our love of sport but to the human need for an ending. The crowning of world leaders is about our restless search for heroes as we discover they are as flawed as the last one and the next one. Like marrying a mistress, appointing a new PM presses the start button on the search for his or her replacement, as indeed my brother wrote in 1997: "Politics is a constant repetition, in cycles of varying length, of one of the oldest myths in human culture, of how we make kings for our societies, and how after a while we kill them to achieve a kind of rebirth."

When the photograph taken inside Buckingham Palace flashed up on-screen and the breaking news alert informed us "BORIS JOHNSON BECOMES PM," I stared in shock at the picture of my brother bowing over the monarch's hand. She stood small but upright in a Brexit Party turquoise dress, black handbag over her left arm, a Dyson Airblade in the corner of the room. Tears prickled at the back of my dry eyeballs. Whether the idea of Boris as PM was your dream or your nightmare, he had done it. I had to hand it to him.

Boris created Brexit. But now he owned it. We are a nation of shopkeepers and therefore the time-honoured high street principle of "you Brexit, you bought it" applied. He would have to do it.

Before he became PM, I was convinced that at least four things would stop Brexit from happening:

pet (and horse) passports
the return of paper international driving licences
roaming charges
Premier League football—one of our most successful
    businesses—being ballsed up by new immigration rules

Above and beyond that, endless faff was set to re-infest so many areas of life that had been frictionless before. I thought that would be the killer. Take, as just one example, standard (as opposed to live or animal) exports to the EU.

As I write, exporters need complete no paperwork or checks as we are in the customs union and single market. After we leave, all roll-on, roll-off locations such as ferry ports will require small export businesses to engage customs agents, apply for movement reference numbers, hire drivers only with specialist goods licences, apply for smart border envelopes, apply for authorised consignor status, buy specialist software to complete customs declarations, train staff to complete specialist customs declarations, complete a combined export and exit summary, make sure that the EU importer has all the necessary licences, numbers, and so on, and keep all the documents pertaining to the export for six years.

Seriously, would businesses bother? Under the new deal,

exporters from the G.B. to Northern Ireland have to complete a fifty-section declaration that apparently takes one and a half hours to fill in. I'd sooner shut up shop. Or move my HQ to the EU. I was convinced that bureaucracy would throttle Brexit at birth. But the election of a true blue Be-Leaver, who spoke of boosterism, Getting Brexit Done, and the U.K. becoming "the greatest country in the world" on a loop made even me doubt my own doubts.

As its author memorably once said, "Brexit means Brexit and we're going to make a Titanic success of it."

. . .

THE NEXT DAY I WOKE UP. MY BEDROOM WAS LIKE AN OVEN. I knew something life changing, something extraordinary, had happened, but it had yet to swim into consciousness. I stuck my feet out from under the duvet to cool them and opened my eyes, and as usual hairy black spiders the size of my fist scuttled across the ceiling. (This is a thing, apparently. I googled it and was disappointed to discover that even my hypnapomic hallucinations are common.)

"Fuck," I said to the ceiling, remembering. "Al is prime minister."

Tweets of the Day:

@TrmarshallTIm Breaking: Rachel Johnson has been appointed Minister of State at the Department for Shrillness and Energetic Hectoring. She will also attend cabinet (obviously).

@imageplotter Breaking: Rachel Johnson crosses back to the Tories and is immediately made new Minister for Change.

@magnesia_London The Johnson family are the pus of British politics. None of them can be trusted. Including Change UK's candidate and biggest mistake Rachel Johnson.

. . .

IT IS TRADITIONAL THAT ALL PMS OR WORLD LEADERS HAVE "entertaining" relations who won't stick to the script and provide light copy for the tabloids. Usually it is a sibling. Terry Major-Ball. Cherie Booth's half sister (sorry, I can't remember her name). Billy Carter.

I could not be more grateful that my father, who in my eyes can do no wrong, has taken on this useful service for the entire family. The fact that my father loves nothing more than appearing on television—and like my nemesis Ann Widdecombe will do any programme with the word "Celebrity" in the title—makes sense of his unilateral decision to be the member of the clan taking one for the team. He is also, let's admit, good copy. In the very week his son became PM, for example, he confided the following:

- He is en route to becoming a French citizen, as his mother had been born in Versailles and his grandmother had been born in Paris. This is good news; I might be able to become French too.
- He couldn't go to a "petit cocktail" hosted by Jean-Claude Juncker for fellow former *fonctionnaires* in Brussels because he was appearing on *Celebrity Gogglebox*.
- He had told Nigel Farage, "I am a Leaver!" in an "exclusive interview" (I love the fantasy that Johnsons can still give exclusive interviews) in which he "switches sides in

the Brexit debate," according to the news story that LBC released later, but would later say on Channel 4 that he was the founder of Environmentalists for Europe, and so on.

Never a dull moment. As he says, "I am a man who on the whole likes to say yes."

Until my father stepped up to the plate, "entertaining relation" was the role I thought I was doomed to play in his premiership, although I had put in an early-bird bid to be the chairman of the Chequers Lawn Tennis Club as my consolation prize for not being elected for anything and not winning anything apart from (1) the Ashdown House Scottish Dancing Cup and (2) the Bad Sex in Fiction Award and (3) *Pointless Celebrities*.

I was so keen to undertake this role that I even went so far as to use Google Earth to check out the gracious country residence of the PM set in the rolling Chilterns. Then I found you can't use Google Earth to view Chequers, so I paged through Google images of the PM's country residence looking for the court. I saw a maze and a little children's playground, a covered pool, gardens. I emailed David Cameron in panic. "Is there a tennis court at Chequers??"

"Yes. A good one. Blair had it resurfaced" came back the instant reply. (DC is very quick off the draw. If someone falls out of the tennis roster and an appeal for a replacement player goes out, he replies within minutes if not seconds.)

I still wake up every morning and wonder if I am dreaming. I wonder if people are giving me a wider berth. I asked my mate the world-renowned *Birdsong* novelist, Sebastian Faulks, to make up doubles; I was desperate for a fourth and knew he was in town. "Sorry," he texted back, "I've emigrated." He did that a few times; then I gave up asking him. Some friends have not called or spoken at all. After a few months, I rang my friend Joy Lo Dico, a writer. "Hello, Joy," I said.

"I haven't dared ring you; it's like ringing someone with cancer," she said as if she were talking to a ghost. "Sorry, you know how it is . . . you don't know how they're getting on and *you don't want to ask.*"

In the family, there is huge pride and amazement, but the under-thirties are a bit weirded out at the combination of the sit-rep: no rulebook for the family plus the Trump playbook for the country. "As a millennial I can confirm there is no social capital whatsoever in Uncle Al becoming PM," one of the cousins announced. "We should at least get a car or a driver or some sort of loyalty card in compensation," my husband moaned.

"Keep notes," the novelist Kathy Lette texted me. "Your life! Some of us have to make this shit up."

.   .   .

IT WILL TAKE A WHILE TO GET USED TO WAKING UP TO THE *Today* programme saying, "The prime minister, Boris Johnson," at the start of every news bulletin. People keep asking me if I will stand in the forthcoming election (I am writing this in early November 2019). I stare at them and shake my head.

What I feel—about standing for election—is this.

It's a bit like the old adage that you should try everything once except incest and Morris dancing. Everyone should at least once in their life. Even if the whole experience is like being picked last for the netball team and it costs an arm and a leg and takes an incalculable toll on your self-esteem, I wouldn't have missed the grisly experience for anything. I yield to no one in my admiration for those who decide to go for it and then stick at it.

All those I know in public service—from local councillors to the first lord of the treasury—deserve medals as far as I'm concerned. They slog away day and night, rain and shine. There's always an election or a candidate to campaign for, a rubber-chicken dinner to be had in some church hall, a school to visit, or a fête to open, and their reward is often obloquy.

The abuse I get online is (so far) tolerable. The two things are related. The reason I don't get abused is that I don't hold public office. As soon as you do, it seems you're fair game. Most candidates spend months, years, coddling their constituencies. The *Spectator* writer and author of *Why We Get the Wrong Politicians,* Isabel Hardman, estimates it costs up to £40,000 to become an MP, which is why we too often get not the right politicians but the rich ones. At the moment very few go unpunished for seeking a life of good deeds and public service.

From the day I became a prospective candidate—St. George's Day, April 23, to Election Day on May 23—my commitment was exactly one month. I gave up a month of my life and my gig on Sky. My cashpoint card stopped working in the hole in the wall. I saw the life of a public servant from the inside, and I knew I couldn't cut it. I didn't have the right stuff. You needed the work rate of an All Black, the hide of a rhino, and the ironclad confidence of David Cameron if you were even going to make it past the selection process, and, above all, you had to believe. Not just in your party, but in yourself. I believed—but not enough.

"Your campaign wasn't so much performance art," said the PM. "It was more . . ." He couldn't think of the right word to express how bizarre the whole thing appeared to the outsider. "I know. Dadaist."

At least it was fast. If you are going to be destroyed at the polling booth, as Macbeth said of murder, "'tis best t'were done quickly." My humiliation—that I couldn't even get myself elected as a lowly Euro MP for Change UK while my brother strolled into Downing Street (Theresa May and Nigel Farage couldn't have done a better job of smoothing his passage if they had rolled out the red carpet themselves)—was land-speed-record quick.

When I went back to *The Pledge* in June, as Toby Sculthorp predicted, instead of getting at least a clap on the back and a "bad luck, old girl," they gave me a T-shirt saying, "46,600 voters CAN be wrong" (it seems incredible, but that was the number of people who voted for me in May 2019), as a booby prize.

"I like you, even if the voters didn't," said Ivo. "You've been fired by everyone, and even the public has sacked you now. It's a badge of honour. Division is celebrated, and you stood against it. If you doubt that, look who was elected president."

It was four weeks that didn't change the world, but perhaps helped smooth the lumpy contours of the British landscape. During those short weeks in the spring and early summer of 2019, we saw a hiatus in the hegemony of two-party politics and the beginning of four-party politics (in local or European elections at least), talk of a national government, the arrival of the Brexit Party, and the revival of the Lib Dems as a threat to Tory autocracy and Labour as the natural party of opposition. We saw the emergence of the most passionate pro-European caucus, paradoxically, in any EU nation, in the U.K. And it has stiffened the EU, not weakened it.

Our rolling maul has provided an effective antidote to Euroscepticism on the Continent, with a record 74 per cent of Austrians, for example, declaring they want to stay in, and Jean-Claude Juncker signing off from his career as a Eurocrat with the words, "Support for the EU is at an all-time high. I chalk this up to Brexit." Another of the unintended ironies of Brexit is that it has made our politics more European. Adonella, the Italian coach of my ladies' tennis team (I'm in the thirds), observed, "You have become like us." In other words: in one bound, the referendum and its long aftermath turned the United Kingdom—for a few months in 2019, anyway—into a cross between Little Italy and *Little Britain*.

·   ·   ·

ON JUNE 4, IT WAS ANNOUNCED THAT CHANGE UK HAD SPLIT, and Chuka had re-re-badged as a Lib Dem. Several others—Wollaston, Allen—followed. The dream of a new Macronesque center party had died. Soubs and Leslie and company fought the 2019 general election but folded the party on December 20. "It was better to have fought and lost than never to have fought at all," Anna Soubry wrote to her loyal but dwindling supporters as an epitaph to her fledgling party that never took flight.

I agree with Anna. I don't think Change UK was for nothing. In a mild way it changed the weather (even if my son Ludo's two suggested titles for this were *How Not to Start a Political Party* and *The Fall—and Fall—of Change UK*).

The start-up was heroic at first, but it morphed too quickly into a suicide mission. I can't say Change UK peaked too soon, because the only peak was on the day it launched. The problem was it happened too soon. Imagine if the twenty-one de-bagged and unwhipped Tories who baulked at a no-deal Brexit had joined forces with the eleven Change UK leaders . . . they would have been a power in the land. But there's no point in crying over spilt milk. "We might get a footnote in a chapter about the Euro elections 2019," said my political guru, Matthew Hooberman, who gave this verdict on the exercise.

"I think 2019 will turn out to be a pivotal year: twenty-one whipless Tory MP Remainers, other Remainer MPs not standing again, eleven Change refugee MPs, and the other independents and peers that left their parties for a Remainer center that

couldn't hold. Did we jump too soon? Why didn't others follow? Why didn't we foresee the Lib Dem local election revival?"

All good questions. It was not to be. The general election
of 2019, in the end, was the curtain-raiser of Tory hegemony
for the foreseeable future. But I still believe—like Matthew
Hooberman—that it had to be done.

I thank the former leaders of the party that was formerly
called the Independent Group and formerly Change UK and
now the Independent Group for Change for taking a chance on
me. Please, then, don't let my failure put you off. I learned a lot.
Not about politics so much as about myself. As we get older,
we reach an accommodation with—and even welcome—our
limitations, but nothing exposes them so expertly as standing
for election.

It does help if you have balls, and you talk balls, as a presenter
of *Woman's Hour* once said. It does help to have the testoster-
onic drive to think that you can do it, too, and want it so much
you are prepared to spend your whole life in preparation for the
moment when the returning officer declares you duly elected.
As a candidate your strengths are taken for granted, but your
weaknesses will be pointed out to you by everyone, because they
are on public display.

.   .   .

AFTER ALL, I HAVE DONE *QUESTION TIME.* I HAVE DONE
Have I Got News for You. I know what happens. I spend the
requisite four hours in hair and makeup, having spent the previous four days trying and failing to think of clever or witty things
to say. The first time I did *HIGNFY,* I made a bad pun. It failed
to raise a laugh, so I said it again. Tumbleweed. "Rachel, a word
of advice," Paul Merton said, leaning over his desk. "If a joke

bombs the first time, don't repeat it." (Roar of laughter from crowd.)

You leave the greenroom, or dressing room, and are shooed into the dark of some large studio and told to mind out for trailing cables. You are lined up in order of entrance. "Break a leg," you whisper to the other panellists politely, but everyone knows this is a contest as brutal and bloody as anything in ancient Rome.

When it's your turn to walk on set, you are patted on the rump by a floor manager with an earpiece, like a dairy farmer sending an unlamented old milker to slaughter. This is your cue to bound in tossing your head like a show pony and take your seat, as if you were enjoying yourself madly already.

I walk in. Wave and smile, beam towards the crowd as a thank-you for turning up. Then the show starts taping, and people realise, after a while, that I am not Boris in a wig. I don't speak in Latin, I don't make jokes about cars and breasts . . . and I lose the room. I don't have the golden stardust, combined with funny bones and borderline genius. "I have forgotten more Greek and Latin than you ever knew," he said to me once, and the fact that it was true made it all the more annoying.

· · ·

AFTER MY BRO BECAME PM (ON DAY ONE HE REVEALED THE Queen had said, "I can't understand why anyone would want this job"), I found myself plagued by this thought sequence. I was the first one to reveal the World King fantasy—that is, the foundational myth of the Johnson rise to power. (I did so in a Michael Cockerell documentary in 2013, which, let the record state, is the only televised interview I have ever done on the subject.) What if he had only said "World King" because he thought, as an eldest son, that was what my father wanted to hear, rather than dustbin man or train driver?

What if he had only said "World King," in other words, for the very same reason that I had said "wife and mother"—that is, gender and birth order—and, from that moment, a terrible Jungian destiny was born, especially as throughout our lives my father tried and failed to become an MP (he even considered throwing his hat in the ring in December 2019 and also once put in for Orpington, the same seat that his son Jo was contesting).

"For as the son of the father, he must, as is often the case with children," said Jung in a key quotation, "re-enact under unconscious compulsion the unlived lives of his parents." It fell to Al, then, to work his socks off and achieve everything my father didn't in politics, and then some. If he hadn't been born first, I'm not sure any of this would have happened.

I have a tendency to think everything is my fault. The corollary of this is I also think everyone blames me for everything. Just one example. When I was en route back from my fateful trip to Jamaica, when I applied to be a Change UK candidate, I was transiting Montego Bay airport with the author Nicholas Shakespeare. We had spent a happy harmonious few days all together, drinking rum, going to plantation houses, eating jerk chicken, and we had just cleared customs and were wandering through the duty-free when he suddenly stood still in the middle of the concourse.

"I can't help it," he suddenly shouted at me, shaking with rage. He dropped his carry-on bag in his toddler tantrum. "It's all you and your fucking family's fault! If none of you EXISTED, we wouldn't be in this terrible mess we are now and I can't forgive you!"

It made me think. What if this partly WAS my fault, if "fault" is the mot juste?

. . .

I REMEMBER SITTING IN THE KITCHEN OF THE FAMILY LONG-house on Exmoor, on a bench at the long table with my back to the Rayburn, and Granny handing me a copy of *The Times* and saying, "Read me the leader while I make the apple crumble." I must have been four or so.

I read it out loud. She turned to Al with her hands in the butter and flour and sugar and said over her specs, "Your sister reads better than you." Granny Butter would take us to a spindly clump of fruit trees down the lane and make us climb them. I would shimmy up using the branches as footholds, and then I would gaze down at her. Granny would be standing far below in her wellies and a dress, with her wild pale hair, the same colour and consistency of the silk you pull off the cob of corn, grinning at me. Another parent would stand in horror wringing their hands but not Granny, a woman for whom no tree was too tall for her then-only granddaughter to climb.

"Higher," she would order, clapping. "Higher!" I would climb higher. With Granny below, I knew I was safe and could not fall.

The other day, someone tweeted out an old interview Al/Boris had done with Elizabeth Day in *The Observer,* in which he talked about our childhood.

He said it was "totally mad but it was wonderful but we were all unbelievably competitive and I owe everything, really, to Rachel and to the arrival of Rachel." I read this with a certain satisfaction as you can imagine, same as when my mother told an interviewer that her firstborn reacted with "shock, disbelief and fear" to my arrival. "If Rachel hadn't appeared when I was fifteen months old, I probably would have lived a life of absolute, total, panda-like passivity and complete acquiescence. I would have just sat there chewing bamboo shoots, doing nothing. . . . And it was the constant struggle for resources, affection, parental time with Rachel—who obviously I'm devoted to—that got me going. So that's all the psychological propulsion you need to discover."

. . .

AL CALLED ME IN JUNE, ON HIS BIRTHDAY. "I'VE BEEN AN MP, I've been mayor twice, I've been foreign secretary, I've edited *The Spectator,* so nobody could accuse me of not doing anything"—and that was BEFORE he became PM.

But.

For the rest of us a bad outcome of all this could be fruit rotting in the fields, gridlock at channel ports, a staffing crisis in social care and hospitals, and a return to the Troubles. For him a bad outcome is the unification of Ireland, an independent Scotland, the dissolution of the United Kingdom, and an abbreviated tenure in Downing Street.

For him, a win is being hailed as the next Churchill and Chequers and a cavalcade of armoured Range Rovers and his photograph on the staircase on the yellow wallpaper of Number 10, next to Mrs. May, a ten-year term. For us, it's clean drinking water, a supply of essential medicines, and sufficient fresh food.

All I can say is it feels as if for him the bar was set high while for the rest of us the bar was low . . . very low.

But who am I to talk? I am a mere virtue-signalling political wind sock, while he is the most powerful man in the country. He is PM, while I am a pub quiz question.

"I love Brexit!" he sometimes says. "I love how it makes everyone go so mad."

Text from Toby Sculthorp, my Sky boss, after Boris had prorogued Parliament and during his first G7 in Biarritz. He had told the Queen he needed to prorogue to prepare for his domestic agenda, but as the supreme court judged unanimously later, the real reason was to nobble the "rebel alliance" and stop them ganging up together to block a no-deal Brexit.

"It's a stroke of genius. He'll go down in history," Sculthorp wrote. "And you'll be a footnote."

After a bit I wrote back, "The punchline, surely?"

When Granny noted that I was reading better than he was, as he said back in June 2010, this galvanised him.

"As the antelope wakes every morning and knows that he must outrun the lion, so I wake every day and know that I must somehow scamper to keep ahead of Rachel," he said.

If this proves anything without doubt, it proves his generosity, his humour, his elastic acceptance of my irritating existence. But if I hadn't been born, he would never have needed to assert his male superiority over me, my siblings, his party—and the rest of the country.

If I hadn't been born, if he hadn't had a pushy little sister snapping at his heels, would he have wanted to be World King? Mmm.

If I hadn't been born, he would probably not be prime minister.

· · ·

AND YET, I DON'T THINK HE EVER CONSIDERED WHAT IT would be like for everyone else, his "loved ones," when he summitted, he podiumed, he lecterned in Downing Street. When you have a brother as famous as he is, and who prefers his limelight neat and undiluted, it changes life for everyone.

When I walk into a pub or restaurant, I see people nudge each other and say in normal voices, "Boris Johnson's sister," without even so much as a hissed "Don't look now, three o'clock. *Sister of Boris*."

When he was mayor, we were all nagged about the siting of London bus shelters; when he was foreign secretary, it was Libya; now that he is first lord of the treasury, I am lobbied on everything by everyone. The editor of *GQ*, Dylan Jones, has been nagging me to get an access-all-areas for the American journalist Michael Wolff to write a long read and book (no doubt to be called *Britain Trump*). He promises it will be a "flatter-a-thon" and sends email chasers to me daily, asking, "What progress?"

I reply, "Dylan. Have you not read *Fire and Fury*?"

A hill farmer on Exmoor called Oliver Edwards who voted for Brexit wants me to tell him when he should sell his lambs. "Just wondering if you have inside info on what sort of £," he texted. "So do I sell lambs in September/October or keep them longer? We usually sell throughout the autumn."

I texted Oliver Edwards saying I was terribly sorry, I didn't know when he should sell his spring lambs. "You voted for this shitshow," I couldn't help reminding him as I thought of all his plump white-fleeced lambs on the hill.

Even my son Ludo has just been Facebooked by a young woman he has met once who is on holiday in the Maldives. The message begins "long time no chat," and then proceeds to ask whether my son can sort out an urgent problem: her boyfriend has by mistake put his passport through the wash and it is not valid. "If you happen to know any trick in the book or any-one in the Peterborough office that could help get his passport renewed . . . ," it ends in wild hope.

· · ·

MY FATHER TAKES HIS BIRTHDAY VERY SERIOUSLY, AND IT is an occasion that he likes to celebrate surrounded by as many of his family as possible. On his sixtieth we gave him a Land Rover on this calculation: What do you give a man who already has a broken-down old Land Rover Defender on his farm? Another broken-down Land Rover Defender!

We celebrated his seventy-ninth at Chequers, the place of rest and recreation for prime ministers forever, set in an idyllic dip of a south-facing shallow valley close to the northern scarp of the Chilterns.

Everyone always asks me what it's been like in the Johnson family post-referendum, what will Sunday lunch and Christmas be like, blah-blah, and then points out, as if we were not all highly aware already of these various schisms, that my father and Jo and I campaigned for Remain, and basically everyone wanted to stay in the EU apart from Boris and my mother (he outed her as a Leaver and his "secret weapon" in his first PM's speech to conference in Manchester). I bat off the answer: I say we don't talk about Brexit at mealtimes because we don't want to gang up on anyone.

I make my stock joke that the family divides into those who think Brexit is a shit idea and those who think it is a really shit idea, but we all get on very well.

It is such fun being together and such a treat that we don't want to ruin it by rowing. Occasionally, life can go a bit boxset (imagine *Succession* meets *Game of Thrones,* location *Chernobyl*)—a brother can resign, a sister-in-law tweets a picture of hell painted by Hieronymus Bosch, a sister can join the Lib Dems or stand for Change UK—but we all abide by the principle that each member of the family has their own inalienable sovereignty. We are free to do and say what we like. By and large, apart from the odd hiccup, mainly on my part, this works.

For the Chequers Stanley Birthday Weekend, I kept driving in circles around Great Missenden. I'd never been before and had no signal and was lost. I was thinking, like Bush at Trump's inauguration, "This is some weird shit," and at length arrived at the designated entry point. This is a heavily protected side drive with fortified entrance and gatehouses, where you have to "park up" before a bombproof barrier. As I did, a pair of coppers with submachine guns and body armour greeted me cheerily. I could glimpse a fleet of police vehicles and black Range Rovers with tinted windows in the cobbled stable yard.

The protection team quickly processed my 2006 Volvo for entry to the historic pleasure ground of PMs past and present, where Heath hosted Nixon; Thatcher, George H. W. Bush; Blair, Putin; and May, Trump. "Been before, Mrs. Johnson?" the coppers asked. The lush grounds unrolled in front of me, and I could glimpse the ruddy Elizabethan façade through trees.

"It's Miss Johnson actually," I said. They radioed to the house. "Two two to three three," he said. A plot started forming in my mind. What if one cop in the ring of steel at Chequers went rogue or was a wrong 'un? And went on a rampage?

A couple came out to greet me as I parked on the scrunchy gravel, and I decided the plot had already been done (*Air Force One*). "Welcome to Chequers," said a Mrs. Danvers in black, smiling, and told me her first name. I was shown to a room with a four-poster bed. Museum-quality paintings on the walls. Deep-carpeted bathroom with chintz furnishings, floral wallpaper. Even toiletries! (There were never any toiletries at Chevening, the country residence of the foreign secretary. Never let it be said I don't endure first-world problems.)

A quick guided tour. Al looked tired and hadn't had a day or even an hour off for months, but bounded around showing us the spread. He said he needed a holiday. "But I can't go abroad," he complained, "because of fucking Brexit!"

There were treasures at every turn. I tried not to seem too keen and impressed. But I was. Be in no doubt. I was THRILLED to be there and all thanks to him. In the great hall there was a massive tooled and brass-knobbed empty chest you could hide many small children in. "It's the James II map chest," said Al.

"It's James I, actually," said a flunkey in RAF uniform.

We passed a cosy study with a knee-hole desk set underneath mullioned windows, armchairs, a fireplace. On a side table an extra-large red box sprawled open containing the secrets of state.

Then a wander round the grounds. "This is where Milo was playing football with Dave Cameron and injured his toe," Al said as we crossed a lawn leading to a ha-ha in front of the house.

Jo and his kids were swimming in the heated pool house ("given by Walter Annenberg in honour of Richard M. Nixon's visit"), but we played tennis on the excellent outdoor court, which had a grey, rubbery, tough all-weather surface—courtesy of Tony Blair. I'd never played on it before but it gave a very true bounce, which is the main thing.

At dinner, the very polite and nice staff addressed my brother as PM ("More lamb, Prime Minister?") rather than Mr. Johnson or Boris. I asked "Mrs. Danvers" why. "We call them all Prime Minister"—then she lowered her voice—*so we don't get their names wrong.*

My father gazed around the scene. We were in the dining room lined with Dutch portraits of slightly thyroidic Flanders mares interspersed with bearded men in ruffs and seascapes in oils. "Chequers on your birthday," I said, as I realised all this was never going to sink in. "What would Granny Butter say?"

"She would be delighted," my father said, in his great-silverback way, "but not surprised."

I thought this:

Dada is seventy-nine. He has a long way to go, but he can go in peace now he has at least one son who is prime minister. Al has given him that. He has made an old man very happy.

The plan had worked.

After dinner (I asked whether the wine came from the cellars but was told it had come from Al's Tesco order; all private hospitality must be paid for by the PM), coffee and special homemade Chequers-branded truffles were served in the Long Gallery: stained-glass windows at one end, fitted bookcases filled with tooled leather-bound tomes, floral sofas facing each other, occasional tables with vases filled with ferns, fireplaces where coal fires burned. Turkish kilims on cream carpets, cream silk ruched lamp shades. The overall impression—warm, creamy elegance and comfort.

I ran my fingers over the silken inlaid surface of Napoleon's desk. "We have his hair too, in the basement, ma'am," said one of the RAF flunkeys.

I admired Cromwell's death mask—the house is crammed with Cromwelliana as one of his grandsons lived here—and the ring that Elizabeth I was wearing when she died, with the aid of a magnifying glass, so I could see with my own eyes two microscopic cameos: one of the queen, the other of her mother, Anne Boleyn.

Nobody slept. I woke at 4:00 a.m. and heard steady trudging in the corridor outside my room. It was either one of the ghosts (Lady Mary Grey was confined here for years for marrying without Elizabeth's consent; there are also tales of a headless horseman) or the protection force on night patrol. At 5:00 a.m. the chorus of wood pigeons that must have been nesting in the ivy or façade began. I lay in a bed of cloud-like softness in a state of disbelief, listening to their coo-cooing.

On my way down to breakfast, I went the wrong way and

found myself in the upstairs cabinet room with its leather-seated carver chairs around a vast oval table. There was a window nook off to one side. Against some wooden panelling I found portraits of the previous incumbents: the Wall of Fame (or Shame, depending on your point of view).

One row, in descending order, black-and-white photographs of Wilson, Heath, Callaghan; next row, Thatcher, Major, Blair. In the third row, in the middle on his own: my sometime tennis partner David Cameron. I took a picture, and sent it to him, thinking he would reply, "Where is Theresa May?" but instead he said, "Where's Gordon Brown?"

Indeed. I therefore asked at breakfast what had happened to Gordon Brown. "Gordon Brown fell off the wall," his successor but three replied.

It was Chequers that made my father, in a state of enhanced, expansive bonhomie, tell me about the email. He'd received it the previous month from a man who said he'd been in Washington with the young Johnson family in 1966–67. My father pinged it on to me with this forwarding message: "I met Adi Davar in Feb 1966. We left Washington for NY in June 1968 so Al in June 1968 would have been four years old."

My dear Stanley,

Pervin and I would like to congratulate you on your son Boris becoming your country's prime minister and on raising a son with his political talents. We wish him and your country under his leadership great wellbeing.

He probably has no recollection now about any of us. But we do and remember him going around as a kid saying I am going to be "a World King." He has now gone

as far as he can and will hopefully steer the UK towards
greater prosperity.

Love, Pervin and Adi

When I read this, forwarded from my father's phone, I almost
sobbed with relief. I hadn't made it up. It wasn't all my fault
after all!

I left Chequers in a hurry to get to the final day of the Test at
Lord's. Al ran after me. Had I left something behind? I always
leave something behind. Mrs. Danvers stood as before waving me off, just as she had greeted me on arrival. "You haven't
signed the visitor's book!"

The last page was opened on the Johnson visit. The leaf
before was a full page of Theresa May's message to the staff. I
read it. It was a sweet, sincere, utterly in character tribute to the
house. "Chequers is a special place but what made it so special
was you, the staff," she wrote, in the tidy hand of a good woman
who had tried her best.

On the page before that, it was Trump. His entry occupied
the whole page. In large black felt tip, he had written a short
message in the middle of the vellum. "It was such an HONOR
to spend some time in your incredible 'HOME,'" he had written. Underneath that, in enormous-point size, his black jagged,
cartoon signature like the trace of someone having a fatal infarct.

"He was quite unsteady on his feet," said Mrs. Danvers, after
I had made my mark in the *livre d'or*. "I had to help him on the
stairs."

When people refer to "your brother," I will always say,
"Which one?" This is a matter of principle.

There is Leo, "the handsome one" (he looks like a cross
between Jeff Bridges and Michael York); there is Jo, "the clever
one" (I had to break Jo had got a first to Al as opposed to our

upper seconds with the words, "Have you heard the terrible news about Jo?" There is always some terrible news about Jo); there is Max, "the tall one." I also have a half sister, Julia—"the kind one"—who teaches, writes, and sings. Max has yet to enter the family business, although he did let slip to the *South China Morning Post* he did not rule it out, but thought the "one out, one in" principle should apply.

There may be an opening for Max, as on September 5, 2019, Jo resigned from the government led by his brother and as an MP for Orpington, citing "unresolvable tensions." I respected his decision. September 5 was a very hard day. The opposition was gifted a killer attack line—"not even his own brother trusts Boris Johnson with the country"—but as usual failed to make much hay with it.

I had to host an awards ceremony in the House of Lords that evening. As I exited, just as I was passing the Greggs in Westminster tube, I heard my name over the Tannoy. "If Rachel Johnson is in the station, please can she make herself known to station staff," a voice said, then repeated it. I thought something terrible had happened, as you would in my shoes, but it was only because I had dropped my credit card as I was "touching out" of the gates.

Several men stopped me in my tracks between the tube and the Black Rod's entrance to pump my hand, and the conversation was always the same.

"Good for your brother!" they would say.

"You mean Jo?" I replied each time, confused, as men and women wrapped in the yellow-starred blue EU flag shouted and waved signs in the background saying, "Bollocks to Boris."

"No. Boris," they each said. "He'll get us out of Europe!"

It's always men who congratulate me on my brother getting Brexit done. I'm afraid I hate being congratulated for this. I would far prefer to be applauded for a sibling who has determined that this country should be part of the EU, outward facing and internationalist, allowing my children the freedom we enjoyed to live, travel, and work in twenty-seven other countries, rather than hunkering down in its rain-girt island fastness.

When men congratulate me, and shake my hand, it always makes me wonder about the election of strongmen across the world. Is the endless stag-do brawl the country has been in since 2016 partly in revenge for #MeToo? Is it because men feel so de-masculinised that they cleave to bragging super-alphas like Trump, Erdogan, Orbán, Bolsonaro, and the others who trample over conventions, norms, and evolved behaviour? Are Brexit and Trump essentially macho, nationalist, willy-waving ("Make Me Big and Hard Again") projects?

Who knows. What I do know is I don't like it when strangers come up and say either "I am relying on you to stop a no deal" *or* "I'm 100 per cent behind Boris." Both statements make me feel disloyal, or guilty, or both.

I made my impeded progress through Westminster to the Cholmondeley Room in the House of Lords for the awards ceremony, where I made limp jokes for money. I said I couldn't keep up with developments in my own close family, let alone politics. It was bad luck about Jo, who had resigned from the government, but at least Dilyn the rescue puppy in Downing Street hadn't defected yet to the Lib Dems.

I joked I would never resign as a sister and was never tempted to take away the whip from myself as a Johnson, even if the sunlit uplands were limited to the Garden of England, Kent, becoming a lorry park for doggers (a throwaway line confirmed by a *Sunday Times* headline of October 6: "Lorry Drivers Stuck in Brexit Traffic Jams May Cause Rise in 'Dogging'"). What I didn't say in the Cholmondeley Room was this: I am so devoted to my brothers that it makes Ivo cross. "I don't know why you don't just marry one of your brothers," he once said.

After the Lords event I went to Emma Barnett's book launch in Soho. It could have been the Bloody Marys, but I found myself bursting into tears, and it was not because I was at a book launch about menstruation and at least one person in the room had sacked me. I suddenly felt tearful at the way Brexit, and politics, was putting a strain on the family. It was getting to the point where it was hard to see whether we would all have Christmas together again.

I hadn't felt so homesick for family, and family life, since I first went to Ashdown aged ten and would lie underneath my pink candlewick bedspread, in the silence in the dark, and pine for my mother. I would suck on a toothpaste tube to quell hunger pangs as tears rolled down my face and I tried to work out how many days it would be until I saw her again—sometimes it was as many as forty-five—and how ill she would be when I did see her.

A general election was called for December. As soon as what became known as the "Brexmas election" was announced, Geordie Greig, the editor of the *Daily Mail,* immediately rang. Would I write a long, intimate, personal piece that explored why, despite our clashing views and the fact we were opposing thumbs politically, I wanted my brother to win a landslide victory. "You're not standing, I take it?" I assured him I would not be. As Al says, politics is brutal and poisonous at the moment— "you have to treat it as if it's a contact sport." I have no urge to do anything except keep my head down.

"It's his Churchill moment," Geordie Greig urged, as he tried to twist my arm to get a double-page, maybe more, spread out of me. "Think about it!"

"Hahaha," I responded.

I emailed David Cameron to ask him to confirm a quotation of his I wanted to use, perhaps as an epigraph for this book, that I couldn't remember exactly. It was about what happened if you challenged an emotional argument with facts and figures. "Can't remember either. The point is that, these days, you lose! Perhaps it was 'logical argument versus emotional argument equals political defeat.'"

Then Cameron went on, "Think Boris will get his majority. Am off canvassing this p.m. Where are you on political journey, Chuck, Libd . . . ? Stand in Kensington as a Johnson-against-Brexit and you would clean up."

"Hahaha," I responded.

Still, clever Geordie had put his finger on something, even though as my editor he tended to demand from me the last piece in the world I wanted to write—that is, the piece that would cause the biggest fallout among my nearest and dearest.

Alexander Boris, Rachel, Leo and Jo in the PM's apartment, 10 Downing Street, February 2020, in front of Charlotte Johnson's painting of Alexander Boris, Rachel, Leo and Jo ca. 1974.

Greig called again in early December. "When are you going to write your piece saying 'Why I Am Voting Tory'?" he demanded.

(Coincidentally, a few days later, over Sunday lunch, my brother urged me to publicly join the Labour Party—his poll lead had at that point narrowed to nine points—as, given my unblemished political track record as reverse Heineken, that would hole them below the waterline. I am, let the record state, unaffiliated with any party and did not campaign in the 2019 GE.)

When I was his lady columnist/pet poodle, Geordie Greig would silkily threaten me with the order of the boot until I delivered what he asked for. We played that game for six years.

But he wasn't my editor anymore. I was no longer on the Associated payroll because the first thing Geordie's successor at *The Mail on Sunday* did before he took over, even before he'd got his feet under the desk, was sack me.

I didn't have to write to order that whatever happened, siblings were bound by blood and soil. I didn't have to tell the readers of the *Daily Mail* that I couldn't help wanting my brother to succeed, because I loved him, as I loved all my siblings. Every cloud, eh.

In the end, as so often, my mother was right.

It was urgent to do nothing.

I have often said Brexit destroys everything in its path, and has divided the country, but it will not break my family.

Just as the cockroaches live on after the nuclear disaster, I must hold on to this, after my laughably brief life in politics.

What will survive of us after Brexit and all that is love.

· · ·

TWEET OF THE DAY FROM ANDREW HOLGATE, THE LITERARY editor of *The Sunday Times:* "Call me selfish, but the number of post-career self-exculpatory political memoirs published in the next year is going to be horrendous."

Email from the American writer and satirist P. J. O'Rourke on the morning of the Tories' landslide victory in the general election, December 13, 2019:

Dear Rachel,

My most sincere congratulations and my most profound condolences on the election of your brother.

Yours,

PJ

Epilogue

Only a short time has passed since one brother resigned from the government led by another, yet it feels like a whole lifetime ago.

I have to keep checking that I stood for the Euro elections not in 2018—nor even in 1988—but in 2019, a few months before the country held a general election called by Prime Minister Johnson, which returned the Conservative government to power in mid-December with a storming majority. A remarkable result, as all agreed, after a decade of Tory-led austerity and more than three even longer years of nonstop internecine bitching about Brexit.

My feelings as I write today are much the same as they were on the morning of December 13, 2019, when, after a sleepless general election night, I sat in a neighbourhood coffee shop in Notting Hill owned by a communist 9/11 denier as the news notifications pinged into my phone, and jotted down these thoughts "in real time":

It's over. His triumph is complete. This is his finest hour. Other leaders across all five continents are hailing the birth of the newborn world king just before Christmas.

Trump arose early from his bed in the White House or Mar-a-Lago (or wherever) to perform his morning tweets.

"Congratulations to Boris Johnson on his great WIN! Britain and the United States will now be free to strike a massive new Trade Deal after BREXIT." (All capitals Trump's own.)

"This deal has the potential to be far bigger and more lucrative than any deal that could be made with the EU. Celebrate Boris!"

Celebrate Boris! Why of course, Mr. President, I do. And I'll tell you why.

Everyone has already pointed out that the Tory victory was built on the "borrowed" votes of Labour voters in the northern industrial heartlands, and the votes of the former red seats had only been lent to the blue team for the duration.

But still. However shaky the foundations of the historic Conservative win, the takeaway from the result was at least window-pane clear. The whole country has heaved a secret or public sigh of relief at the main campaign promise that we would never have to talk about Brexit again.

My side had been vanquished. The Remain cause had been lost, lost utterly. Every single Change UK MP lost their seat and left Parliament. It would take twenty years and a younger, more determined generation to take us back into the EU. My children would spend their productive lives as British subjects, not European citizens with the freedom of twenty-seven other countries at their feet. I'll admit: it still hurt.

That moment before Christmas in Coffee Plant, on the Portobello Road, marked a milestone for me. I wasn't going to fight yesterday's battles, not the way that cookie had crumbled.

As promised, on January 31, 2020, the U.K. left the EU at the stroke of 11:00 p.m., and we entered a transition period. Big Ben didn't bong us out, as it was under reconstruction, but the government marked the caesura in our island story by beaming a virtual Big Ben onto Number 10 to chime. A few hundred yards away, in Parliament Square, Nigel Farage led a seething, flag-waving throng in a rousing chorus of "God Save the Queen" to mark what he said was "the single biggest moment in the history of our country."

. . .

AS I WANDER THROUGH WESTMINSTER DURING THIS SOGGY English spring of 2020 (this February was the wettest on record), and I half close my eyes, I can still see and hear the ghosts of the battle that was fought there, 2016–19, so seared is it onto my weary consciousness.

I see the English nationalists for whom Brexit is rapture in Union Jack hats duelling with the European activists for whom it is rupture waving their blue-and-gold banners and shouting into megaphones.

I see the broadcasters' white marquees set up in College Green for politicians and talking heads to dissect every jot and tittle of the withdrawal agreement, or the parliamentary votes for them or against them. It all went on so long everyone assumed it would go on forever.

Brexit was a process, not an event, everyone said, including me, and this "civil war without the muskets"—as one newspaper editor put it—would see us all out.

And then—at the general election, just before Christmas—it stopped. And there was this eerie silence.

Other anxieties, of course, have crowded in to fill the unaccustomed vacuum as the year marches on.

The Labour Party continues to destroy itself. The Conservative Party continues to declare that anything, however stupid and self-destructive and costly (leaving the European bodies that regulate and monitor and exchange data on medicines, aviation, counterterrorism), is a price worth paying for independence and sovereignty. Ideology continues to drive decision making. The human race continues to degrade the planet.

And then, just when it didn't seem possible that one country could self-isolate even more than the U.K. already had, came the pandemic of COVID-19—coronavirus.

The world started panic buying hand sanitiser and toilet rolls, and everyone felt as if they were living through the first ten minutes of a disaster movie.

In response, I decided it was time, after five years of mourning for my Lab-collie crossbreed Coco, to get another dog. I put a deposit down on a blond, curly-haired cockapoo bitch from a breeder not far from us in Somerset who spoke about worming pills and injections with a reassuring West Country accent.

On the morning of March 10, I played tennis with the former British PM David Cameron and gave him an advance copy of this book and quickly showed him pictures of the cockapoo litter on my phone to distract him from reading it, but as it turned out, he was not my target audience.

"My mother-in-law feeds her dogs from the table," he said, after a cursory glance at the blond fur and melting eyes and bumbling paws, "and it torments me so much I lie in bed working out how to exterminate not just her dogs *but all dogs in central London.*"

Later the same day, as he started to read this book, I got a series of texts objecting to my harsh analysis of his decision to call the referendum, to which I replied.

He made it clear that he hated what happened with the referendum, but felt he had no choice but to call it (he argued it was a manifesto pledge for which nine out of ten MPs had voted).

We were both defensive, we both stuck to our guns, but then we couldn't fight about it anymore.

In fact, we couldn't bear to even discuss it anymore.

"I actually think it is better now," Cameron texted. "Election was decisive. Brexit argument virtually over (totally over outside London). People thinking about Corona, future, dogs, etc."

I sent him a picture of my intended puppy with no name as a teasing peace offering, even though he had said that morning that if the British public knew the extent to which he was "not a dog person," he would never have been elected PM.

"When my daughter is stressed, she looks at cat pictures on the internet," he said.

That's where we are, then. Looking at cat pictures on the internet as we face the calamity of coronavirus and try, in our phlegmatic British way, to keep calm and carry on.

Consummatum est. It is finished.

Time to drive west to see a man about a dog.

London, March 10, 2020

ACKNOWLEDGEMENTS

This book would not have been published without the discernment and faith of my publishers, Ian Marshall of Simon & Schuster and Victoria Wilson of Knopf, and the dogged support of my agents, Georgia Garrett of RCW in London and Melanie Jackson in New York.

Melissa Bond and Lindsay Davies coped with the subbing and proofs, which went right up to the wire into 2020. Matthew Hooberman made me take out yet more mentions of David Cameron and tennis and also flagged up "pointless name-dropping" and "more showing off" with his merciless neon highlighter, and he was right every time. George Foote from Sarah Wollaston's office was very helpful with data and polls, and Catherine Faulks with Tory selection procedures.

I'd also like to thank John Witherow, the editor of *The Times,* and Geordie Greig, the editor of the *Daily Mail,* for ordering me to get the book done, even though I sometimes have to remind them I am no longer on payroll.

Last, but most important, I would like to thank my family for their indulgence—and forgiveness—if I've written anything in the heat of the moment and in virtual real time they don't like or agree with or I've got wrong. I'm sure I have, and my apologies in advance.

In the meantime, let the healing continue!

INDEX

Page numbers in *italics* refer to photographs.

A NOTE ON THE TYPE

The text of this book was set in Simoncini Garamond, a modern version by Francesco Simoncini of the type attributed to the famous Parisian type cutter Claude Garamond (ca. 1480–1561). Garamond was a pupil of Geoffroy Tory's and is believed to have based his letters on the Venetian models, although he introduced a number of important differences, and it is to him we owe the letter that we know as old style. He gave to his letters a certain elegance and a feeling of movement that won for their creator an immediate reputation and the patronage of Francis I of France.

Composed by North Market Street Graphics,
Lancaster, Pennsylvania

Printed and bound by Friesens,
Atona, Canada

Designed by Betty Lew